6/08

Henderson

WITHDRAWN

Unyielding Spirit,

the history of the Polish people of St. Louis

by NiNi Harris

ISBN: 978-0-9794985-0-3

©2007 by NiNi Harris. All Rights Reserved.

Published and distributed by
St. Stanislaus Kostka Parish, Saint Louis, Missouri, USA

Unyielding Spirit,
the history of the Polish people of St. Louis

~ Table of Contents ~

Introduction

The nation of Poland was only a memory and a dream when its sons and daughters began settling in St. Louis to build new lives, homes and communities.

In 1791, Polish patriots and revolutionaries had authored the most democratic of constitutions. Four years later, the powerful European empires — threatened by such democratic philosophy — squelched that revolutionary movement, and dismantled a budding republic in Poland. They divided the nation like loot, erasing Poland from the map for 124 years.

The Austrian Empire, with its polyglot of ethnic groups, took Southern Poland and inflicted its laws and language on the people. Czarist Russia cruelly dominated eastern Poland. Prussian-Germany sought to wipe out the Polish language, customs and Polish character in the west of Poland.

Though divided and occupied by the German, Russian and Austrian empires, the identity and culture of Poland lived in its people's hearts. Despite division and oppression at home, the Polish immigrants maintained and restored their distinctive culture and their Roman Catholic religion in St. Louis.

In 2005, 170 years after the beginnings of a Polish community in St. Louis, the parishioners of the only Polish Roman Catholic church remaining in St. Louis took a stand in opposition to the Archbishop of their Archdiocese over property ownership. They were condemned by some. Their parish leadership was excommunicated. National media — CBS, the New York Times, the Wall Street Journal — reported their struggle and their defiance to the Roman Catholic Church.

The history of these Polish - Catholics, as a community and as individuals, in Europe and in America, their struggles to preserve their culture, their religious beliefs, and their property — did not allow them to yield.

Individuals

Over a thousand people jammed onto the 1400 block of North 20th Street to see the cornerstone of the first Polish Catholic Church lowered into place on Sunday, July 16, 1882. The *St. Louis Globe-Democrat* described the jam as, "frightful, a good many women and children receiving a severe squeezing before being able to extricate themselves." Five bands — German and Bohemian — participated in the celebrations. More than a dozen church dignitaries, German, Bohemian and Irish, joined the Polish-St. Louisans in the ceremonies and celebration.

That moment in history not only initiated the building of the first Polish Parish in St. Louis, it also marked the beginning of a distinctive Polish community in the gateway city. That unique community would build its own neighborhoods, develop its own social life, celebrate its own holidays and feast days, and would enrich the character of St. Louis.

Though that late, summer afternoon in 1882, was a seminal moment for the creation of a Polish community, there had already been a Polish presence in St. Louis for half a century.

A handful of Polish individuals — emigres and exiles — had settled in antebellum St. Louis. These individuals were both admired and the source of fascination in the young, American city.

▼ The St. Louis riverfront as it appeared in the early 1830's, when Polish patriots and exiles began arriving in the frontier metropolis. The image is a copy of a painting by L.D. Pomarade that was published in *Compton & Dry's Pictorial St. Louis*.

At that time, St. Louis was a frontier metropolis full of energy, traffic, and building. Its riverfront was funneling explorers, soldiers, settlers, missionaries,… to the American West. Waves of people — Creoles, Early Americans, Irish, Germans, Bohemians, African-Americans both free and enslaved — were building St. Louis during the first half of the 19th century.

Arriving in St. Louis in 1834, John K. Rychlicki was one of the first Poles to adopt the frontier city as his home. The son of landed gentry and a graduate of the University of Warsaw, he had refused an appointment to the high court. Instead, he joined the Polish patriots in the revolution to overthrow the Russian colonial government in eastern Poland in 1831. Rychlicki fought for nine months for the liberation of Poland. After the Russian Army defeated the patriots, the Polish revolutionaries retreated to Galicia, the southern part of Poland under Austrian control. There they remained for two years, surrounded by the Austrian Army. Pressured by the Russians, the Austrians expelled the patriots. "John K. Rychlicki was one of the 600 who chose the United States as the place of exile, and who were brought over to this country in three Austrian frigates," Walter Stevens wrote in his history of St. Louis in 1909.

After a short stay in New York, where he tutored in Latin and Greek, Ryclicki traveled west. Crossing the country by stage to St. Louis took three months. He arrived in frontier St. Louis in September of 1834. His second day in town, he found a job as a civil engineer, working alternately in the surveyor general's office and in the field, surveying public lands.

Major William Clark Kennerly, St. Louis nephew of the great explorer William Clark of the Lewis and Clark expedition, made reference to another early Polish settler. In his memoirs, Kennerly wrote that in 1834, "we had our first lessons in fencing, from Rooskooski (maybe Ruszkowski) a Pole, who filled the position of valet to General Clark after the death of his faithful (servant) Yorke. He had been in the army of his own country and was an expert swordsman, …"

The limited evidence of the early Polish settlers is confused by Anglicized spellings or two and three different spellings of the same name, as in the case of "Napoleon Koscilowski."

Napoleon Koscilowski appears in the 1845 St. Louis City Directory as an engineer living on the west side of 10th Street, near Market Street. The following year war broke out between the United States and Mexico, and Napoleon Koscialowski, with an extra vowel and an extra syllable in his last name, appears in accounts of the local war effort. In response to the Governor's request for volunteers to serve during the war, it was reported that the Kosciusko Guards were organized by June 9, 1847. It was also reported that Napoleon Koscialowski was elected captain of the Kosciusko Guard. After the war, Koscialowski served on a committee to welcome home veterans of the War with Mexico.

Failed revolutions in Eastern Europe in 1848 brought many new German, Austrian and Bohemian immigrants to St. Louis. In the years that followed the revolutions, small numbers of Poles also arrived in St. Louis, via New Orleans.

The 1850 federal census listed at least 81 residents of St. Louis who claimed Poland as their birth place. The census shows 40 year-old Ed Pulkowski, born in Poland, working as a peddler living south of Downtown. Only

▲ This portrait of John Rychlicki, an exiled Polish patriot who adopted St. Louis as his new home, appeared in the Encyclopedia of the History of St. Louis, published by William Hyde and Howard Conard in 1899.

four years later, an Ed Polkowski is listed as owning a dry goods store on Broadway and residing on the east side of 7th Street in the Frenchtown neighborhood. The city directory lists Charles Kasminski working as a shipping clerk and living on the northern edge of Downtown.

During the early 1850's, and while continuing to hold his position as a civil engineer in the surveyor general's office, John Rychlicki opened his own civil engineering office on North Broadway between O'Fallon and Cass Avenues. Stevens described Rychlicki as, "a splendid representative of the Polish element in the community, …"

Among the Poles settling in antebellum St. Louis was a chemist. A federal census worker, struggling to understand and spell the Polish names phonetically, recorded the chemist's name as "Robert Comassa." Though the Polish immigrant could not find work as a chemist locally, he found that his skills were useful in a different, local enterprise — distilling liquor for a riverfront tavern known as the General Zachary Taylor House.

On a Saturday evening in May of 1860, the "justly renowned Polish fencer and teacher, Mr. Constantine Blandowsky," presented a "Tournament of Military Arms" at the Turnverein Hall on 10th Street between

Market and Walnut Streets. An article promoting the tournament in the May 12, 1860, issue of the *Missouri Democrat* stated, "We have on several occasions witnessed the masterly skill with which Mr. Blandowsky wields a rapier, broadsword or gun and bayonet."

According to the *Missouri Democrat*, he possessed, "extraordinary skill in fencing, and has taught the art to many large and highly respectable classes, both in St. Louis and elsewhere."

Blandowski, as his name was usually spelled, was born in 1821 in Poland. He received a military education and became a soldier. "In the revolutionary movements of Poland, and also of Hungary he actively participated, as well as in the war of the Crimea."

He visited cities in the United States, and traveled to the Rocky Mountains and the valley of the Yellowstone River. His trip west was with the great American painter, Carl Wimar, who painted Blandowski's portrait. In St. Louis, the Polish emigre married an immigrant from Prussia, and they started a family. By 1860, Blandowski and his wife Sophia had two daughters. The federal census listed Blandowski's profession as a "dance master."

Another native of Poland, Eduard Sobolewski, became prominent in the arts in antebellum St. Louis.

Born in Kolobrzeg in 1808, by 1817 Sobolewski had played the violin in the theater orchestra at Krolewiec. In the 1820's, he studied in Dresden with German composer Carl Maria Friedrich von Weber. Later he returned to Krolewiec, where he established a musical academy and taught singing. Franz Liszt invited him to conduct at Weimar. Liszt also conducted Sobolewski's original work at Weimar. In 1859, Sobolewski moved to the United States, first establishing and conducting an orchestra in Milwaukee. He left that new orchestra to help establish the Saint Louis Philharmonic.

Eduard Sobolewski lifted the baton at 7:45 p.m. on Thursday, October 18, 1860, to conduct the first performance of the St. Louis Philharmonic. The setting was the Mercantile Library Hall, at Broadway and Locust Streets in Downtown St. Louis. The Polish conductor stood before the concert orchestra and a 70 voice chorus, in a program that included not only orchestral and choral selections, but also a piano concerto by Beethoven.

Only 20 days earlier, the Board of the new St. Louis Philharmonic had hired Eduard Sobelewski as its first musical director.

For the annual salary of $1,000, Sobolewski was to reserve one evening each week for chorus rehearsal, one each week for orchestra rehearsal, and three to four hours a day for instruction with individual musicians.

The St. Louis Daily News covered Sobolewski's first concert in St. Louis and reported, "The Philharmonic Concert last evening was a decided success. Little did we expect to hear such a good and complete performance after so short a period of the Society's existence…"

Though Sobolewski's work was reviewed in the local newspapers, apparently he was overlooked by the federal census of 1860.

The census tabulated the population of the City of St. Louis at 160,773, documenting that the city had more than doubled in size in a mere decade. The federal census recorded a small number of Poles living in St. Louis in 1860, but no Sobolewski. During his move, the Polish composer and conductor may have missed both the census takers in Milwaukee and in St. Louis.

At least 144 St. Louisans told census takers that their birthplace was Poland. The skills and background of the census taker often influenced the entries. Evidently one census taker was German, because he wrote the birthplace of Polish born residents as "Polen," the German spelling of Poland. Often the new immigrants did not know how to spell their names in English, and the census taker anglicized, unintentionally disguising, the Polish names. For instance, in the 1860 census last names for some individuals born in Poland were recorded as King, Smith, Marks and Davies — common Anglo names. Other last names appeared German, like Kreiger and Weber. These names could have belonged to Germans born in Polish territory. Or the names could have resulted from decades of German domination of western Poland, during which time many Polish names were transformed into German names.

Despite the spellings, and faded handwriting making some parts of entries illegible, the 144 entries clearly giving Poland as birthplace offer a wealth of information.

In 1860, Polish-born St. Louisans were living in every one of the city's 10 wards. Each ward formed a corridor from the river to the city's western boundary, which approximately followed Grand Avenue.

A total of 76 Polish-born St. Louisans lived in the wards that included parts of the densely developed and busy downtown area. The highest concentration was on the northern edge of Downtown. The second highest concentration, 26, was in the ward that included the northern section of the Soulard or Frenchtown neighborhood.

Only six Polish-born St. Louisans lived in the northern third of the city, north of O'Fallon Avenue, which would have been largely undeveloped at that time. Only eight Polish-born St. Louisans lived in the entire area of the city south and west of Soulard Market, which also had a rural character in 1860.

These St. Louisans of Polish ancestry pursued a wide variety of trades to earn their living. One was listed as a medical doctor and another as an architect. Two said they made their living as a "riverman," perhaps roustabouts on the paddle wheelers or the wharves. A handful listed their work as "laborer." One of these laborers worked at the U.S. Arsenal, at the south end of the Soulard or Frenchtown neighborhoods. The role of immigrants in the St. Louis workforce of 1860 is clear from the fact that the list of laborers at this largest federal arsenal in the American West included not only a Polish-American, but also numbers of immigrants from Scotland, Ireland and Germany.

Many new, single immigrants lived in boarding houses. One Polish immigrant, living in a boarding house, worked as a "City Marshal."

Some of the immigrants were tradesmen. Their ranks included carpenters, glaziers, sign painters, a tinsmith, a coppersmith and a teamster.

At least seven Polish immigrants were laborers in the tobacco industry. This work would have probably been exceptionally low paying, since this industry included many slaves in its workforce.

The beginnings of St. Louis' garment district is also reflected in the jobs found by these early Polish immigrants. Their ranks included at least three milliners, two shoemakers, two dressmakers, two tailors and a capmaker. Polish-born merchants, clothiers, and clerks helped with St. Louis commercial life. The census listed a least 14 peddlers and two hucksters among the Polish-born in St. Louis. This demanding work often paid little. But it also proved a stepping stone for many hoping to eventually own a business or shop. Polish women also found work as servants or as cooks.

The census reported one Polish-born St. Louis resident as a musician, one a sexton, one a horse trader and one a chemist. The Polish-born newspaper carrier, however, appeared more prosperous than most of his peers. The value of his real estate was estimated at $1,100.

A few Poles lived in nearby Carondelet, a few more in Manchester, at least one listed his residence at Jefferson Barracks, and more were scattered around current St. Louis County.

In the winter of 1860-61, the United States of America was breaking apart, as southern states that allowed slavery were seceding from the Union. While many in the State of Missouri sympathized with the seceding slave states, the immigrants from Central Europe secured St. Louis for the Union.

After Confederate forces fired the opening shots of the Civil War, attacking Fort Sumter on April 12, 1861, St. Louisans answered Abraham Lincoln's call for volunteers.

Polish-born Ladislaus Koniuszeski became a Captain in Rifle Company A of the First Regiment Infantry Missouri Volunteers. Koniuszeski turned 27 during the first year of the Civil War. He had lived with his family on Myrtle Street, and worked in the "lottery office" located at Second and Walnut Streets on the riverfront. His family estimated their personal estate at $1,000.

Koniuszeski's regiment was complete by April 27th and elected Francis P. Blair their colonel.

Polish patriot Constantin Blandowski

earned the rank of captain of Company F, in the almost entirely German Third Regiment Infantry, Missouri Volunteers. At the end of April, the regiment was completed, with Francis Sigel as colonel.

Other names like Anton Adamski, Jonas Kalinovski and Joseph Stankowsky appear in the ranks of St. Louis' volunteers for the Grand Army of the Republic in the spring of 1861. There were estimates that as many as 200 St. Louis Poles enlisted in the Union Army during the Civil War. Since there were so few Polish-born St. Louisans at that time, this number seems exaggerated. However, it may have included Poles from surrounding counties who enlisted in St. Louis.

In the spring of 1861, federal troops guarded the federal arsenal on South Broadway and many more were stationed at Jefferson Barracks, south of St. Louis City. The Missouri Militia, which sympathized with the Confederacy, was camped in Lindell Grove, around Grand Avenue and Lindell Boulevard. Their camp was named Camp Jackson in honor of Missouri Governor and Confederate sympathizer Claiborne Jackson.

On May 10, 4,000 Federal troops mobilized at the arsenal. Regulars and new recruits, they marched to Camp Jackson, surrounded it, and took the Confederate militia members prisoner.

As the Union troops marched these Confederate prisoners, across the city to the Arsenal, crowds of Confederate sympathizers gathered. They taunted and jeered the Federal troops. They derided the German-American troops, calling them the "Damn Dutch" or Deutch. Accounts of the march may have varied — stones were thrown, a drunk in the crowd shot at soldiers — but all the accounts described an ensuing riot.

Someone in the crowd shot Union Captain Blandowski, wounding him in the leg. Then Federal troops fired into the crowd, killing 28 civilians.

The *Missouri Democrat's* account stated, "Capt. Blandowski, who was without provocation assaulted and shot in the leg while commanding his company at Camp Jackson, …"

On May 23, Blandowski's wounded leg was amputated in an attempt to save his life. The surgery, however, "proved too severe a shock for the patient's diminished strength. He sank soon after the amputation of his leg,…and shortly afterward expired," the *Missouri Democrat* stated.

Though the Polish patriot had lived in St. Louis only a few years, the great respect this community held him in was demonstrated by his funeral.

At 7:30 a.m. on May 27, his funeral procession formed in front of the Good Samaritan Hospital, on 24th Street between Cass Avenue and O'Fallon Street in North City. Mounted Orderlies lead the funeral procession. A funeral escort, a band, the coffin, Blandowski's Company F, carriages carrying relatives, then carriages transporting United States Army officers and officers of the United States Reserve Guards, and members of the Turnverein (a German gymnastic association) followed. The funeral cortege also included officers and non-commissioned officers of at least four more companies and twelve carriages transporting citizens.

The cortege led to Picket's German Protestant Cemetery on Gravois Road, where Blandowski was laid to rest with military honors.

Union General Nathaniel Lyon helped establish a fund in behalf of Blandowski's widow and three children.

Through that anxious winter and early spring leading to the war, Eduard Sobolewski and the Philharmonic Society had continued to lift people's spirits and enrich their lives. They presented eight concerts. That they were meeting a need in the community was evidenced by the attendance. An average of 1,255 people attended each of the concerts.

The orchestra's financial resources were limited by the outbreak of the Civil War. His second season, Soboleski accepted a pay cut. As the war continued, another challenge was created for the Polish director and his orchestra. New musicians had to be trained, to replace those who had left to join the Army. Sobolewski and the Philharmonic continued to present concerts.

In 1863, resources in St. Louis, as in the rest of the nation, were stretched. Public and private buildings were converted into hospitals for Union soldiers wounded in the Siege of Vicksburg. Though St. Louis was playing a strategic role for the Union in the western theater of the war, skirmishes were still being fought all over Missouri.

In the midst of all this turmoil, Polish-St. Louisans formed a National Committee to support the struggle to liberate the Polish homeland. John Rychlicki joined the committee. By the end of the year, the committee was able to send $6,000 to Poland to aid the Insurrection of 1863. After the collapse of the Polish revolution, the committee went out of existence. It appears that many of the St. Louis Poles moved on at that time — to agricultural communities outside St. Louis.

During 1863-1864, a missionary from Texas, Father Leopold Moczygeba, served the spiritual needs of the Poles in St. Louis.

When General Robert E. Lee surrendered the Army of Virginia at Appomatox, St. Louis was energized with returning soldiers and new immigrants. By 1870, the federal census reported the population of St. Louis had again doubled, to more than 310,000 people. The citizenship included more than 59,000 German-born and more than 32,000 Irish-born St. Louisans.

By comparison, only 300 St. Louisans were born in Poland. Though small in number, these immigrants combined with second generation Polish Americans in St. Louis formed the seed of a community — adding their customs and traditions to the cultural mix of St. Louis.

That year, 16-year-old Julius Trojanowski emigrated from Russian ruled Poland. Before long he was living on the near South Side of Downtown and had found work in one of St. Louis' many shoe factories.

During the early and mid-1870's, visiting priests served the small Polish community in St. Louis. In 1878, Father Anthony Klawiter from New Posen, Nebraska, held a mission for the local Poles. He suggested they organize their own Roman Catholic Parish and build their own church in their adopted city.

After two weeks of canvassing, the results were meager. Thirty-seven Poles had signed up for their new parish. Their assets amounted to $33.00. With permission from the Archdiocese, the Poles held masses in the basement of St. Joseph's at 11th and Biddle Streets, on the north edge of downtown. Their singing, however, interfered with services on the main floor. The Poles were asked to leave. An Irish Parish, St. Lawrence O'Toole founded in 1853, then welcomed the Polish congregation. The Poles met in the parish school at O'Fallon and 14th Streets.

During the mid-19th century, individual Poles had made their way to St. Louis and added to the richness of community life. The forming

▲ The Eads Bridge spanned the Mississippi by the time this engraving was published in 1876 in Compton & Dry's Pictorial St. Louis. The Western Engraving Company depicted both the heavy river traffic and the smokestacks rising above the City's near north side in this image.

of a parish indicates that the random emigration was growing into a stream of Polish immigrants.

Joseph Olszewski and his family members had traveled to Venezuela, and then returned to Poland. Their home in Poland was ruled by Germany. The German military draft threatened the boys of the family. Members of the Olszewski family decided to permanently move to the United States about 1878. To flee the draft, they traveled at night, and hid in haystacks during the day. Then they sailed for New Orleans. One brother died before reaching St. Louis. Once here, they settled on North 10th Street.

The Olszewski family, however, were not the only Poles to settle in St. Louis, after first exploring the possibilities in South America. Forty new Polish families arrived in St. Louis, via South America, in the summer of 1879. They had been lured to South America by publicity describing Brazil as "the land of milk and honey." Disillusioned and disappointed at the reality of working on the sugar plantations, they sailed for New Orleans, and from there made their way upriver to St. Louis. Their hardships were multiplied by yellow fever.

Among those reaching St. Louis were Joseph Murawski, Casimir and John Kalinowski, August and Francis Marchlewski, Thomas Wisniewski, Joseph Mitulski, and Thomas and John Lubiewski.

With the arrival of the Karakasy, the Poles who emigrated via Caracas, St. Lawrence O'Toole's school was no longer large enough for the Polish congregation's masses.

St. Patrick's school basement became the next chapel for the Polish Catholics. Located at Sixth and Biddle Streets, the parish which had served Irish Catholics since its founding in 1848 was more convenient for the Poles. It was near the Ashley Building, a four-story tenement that covered half a block fronting Third Street between Ashley and O'Fallon Streets. This tenement — near the riverfront, railroad tracks and industry — at any given time housed over 600 individuals, most of them recently arrived immigrants.

Each Sunday, the Poles walked in a procession from the Ashley Building to St. Patrick's Church. Father Bradley, who lived at St. Patrick's Parish as a boy, recalled the

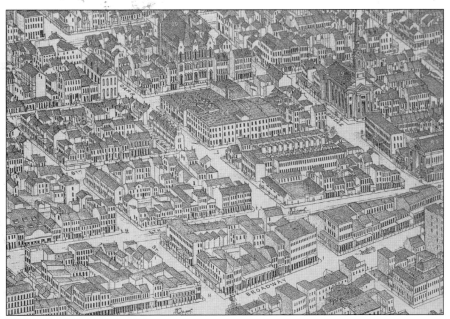

◀ The Poles paraded by Greek Revival style St. Patrick Church, at 6th and Biddle Streets, on their way to mass in the chapel in the basement of St. Patrick School. The three and one-half story school building towered over the surrounding rowhouses, stores and factories on 7th Street near Biddle Street, in this lithograph from Compton & Dry's Pictorial St. Louis.

weekly parades of the Poles, "dressed in their European costumes of many colors." He stated that, "this spectacle offered the Irish denizens plenty of entertainment, on the whole it was edifying to see them (the Poles) practice their religion so openly."

These colorful processions — through the drab and gloomy streets lined with tenements — continued the whole time the Poles worshipped at St. Patrick Parish.

Father Klawiter opened the first Polish School in St. Louis, operating at St. Patrick's Parish. Father Sebastian Cebula replaced Klawiter. The Polish Catholics held a picnic in June of 1879 to raise money to build a new altar for their basement chapel.

At that time, the city was becoming more American. In 1880, the population increased to over 350,000 people, while the total number of foreign born decreased to about 105,000 people. Clearly, the second generation Germans and Irish were beginning to play a larger role in St. Louis.

The number of Polish-born St. Louisans increased slightly to 389. The Polish community, however, was on the verge of dramatic growth.

Community

The purchase of a site to build a Polish church at 20th Street and Cass Avenue spurred the development of a distinct Polish community. The site would become the center of church life, community life and social life. It would give rise to a Polish neighborhood surrounding it.

The lots for the church, purchased in 1880, cost $4,864. At that time, however, the concentration of the Polish settlement was not near the new church site. It was to the east, near the industrial jobs along North Broadway and along the river. But this site on 20th Street near Cass Avenue offered the room to grow.

The site on 20th Street was in a neighborhood of brick mansions and frame shanties, a community of Irish ditch diggers and German brewers, an area of crowded apartment buildings, churches, schools, box factories, and of ponds, creeks, and large open spaces.

The block chosen for the parish was mostly open land.

German and Irish-Americans were building along the major nearby street, Cass Avenue. Even when they constructed the early, scattered buildings, these new St. Louisans were clearly envisioning a busy city neighborhood.

Building permits document the physical character of the developing neighborhood.

By the time of the dedication of the original St. Stanislaus Church, the City had issued permits to construct three-story brick buildings on the 2000 block of Cass Avenue, around the corner from the church property. Storefronts filled the first floors of the buildings and apartments were on the second and third floors. The City had also issued permits to construct two-story townhouses on this block of Cass.

Though there is little evidence of buildings

immediately around the church site on 20th Street, nearby was a busy community life.

German St. Vincent Orphan Home operated out of a three story building a few blocks to the east of the church site, on Hogan Street. St. Vincent's, located there since 1851, provided home, yard and garden space for the children.

Within a few blocks of the church site, the huge Visitation Convent covered an entire block facing Cass Avenue. Adjacent to the convent, stood the magnificent home of James Clemens, Jr., at 1849 Cass Avenue. Irish St. Louis architect, Patrick Walsh, designed the Greek revival style mansion, with extraordinary cast iron columns and ornament, in 1858. Clemens died at age 87, and his heirs sold the grand home to the Sisters of St. Joseph.

▼ Fields and ponds surrounded the rowhousese and shanties that stood in the area around 20th Street and Cass Avenue. The three-story St. Vincent German Orphan Home is at the bottom and the Convent of the Visitation at the right side of this drawing from Compton & Dry's Pictorial St. Louis.

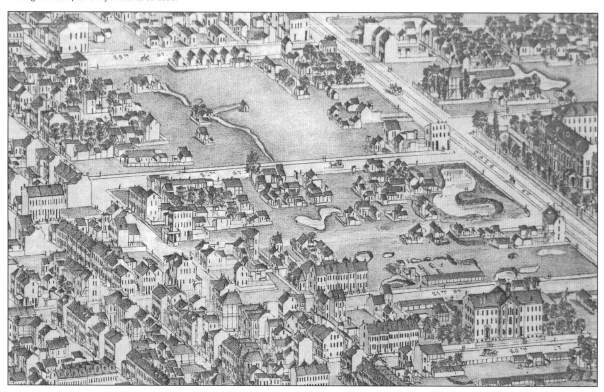

The second-empire style Brinckwirth mansion faced Cass Avenue on the east side of the Clemens mansion. The German-American Brinckwirth family had made their fortune with Brinckwirth Nolker Brewery.

Brick rowhouses, schools, stores and industries filled many of the blocks to the south and east of the parish lots.

Nearby, scattered and surrounding the site of the new Polish Parish, was Kerry Patch, an area settled by Irish fleeing the potato famine of the 1840's. The impoverished Irish had squatted on what was then part of the city commons, land owned by the City of St. Louis. They built shanties without knowledge of where streets were planned. The Irish men of "Kerry Patch are laboring men, who, for the price of a couple months' rent of rooms, have obtained the material with which they

▼ The Clemens Mansion on Cass Avenue as shown by Compton & Dry's Pictorial St. Louis.

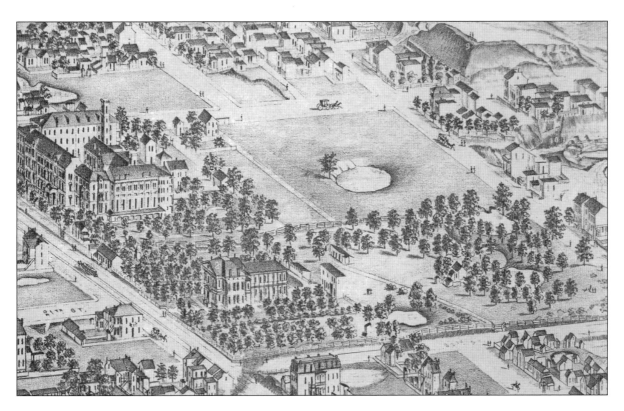

constructed dwellings, which have served them and their families for five, six and seven years," wrote St. Louisan J.A. Dacus in 1878.

According to Jack Sheehan, who was known as the last "King" of Kerry Patch, originally Kerry Patch covered the territory bounded by 16th Street on the east, 19th Street on the west, O'Fallon Street on the south and Cass Avenue on the north. Later, others defined Kerry Patch as spreading farther east and farther south.

Early Roman Catholic Churches also define a general Irish settlement area that would have included Kerry Patch. In addition to St. Patrick and St. Lawrence O'Toole parishes, St. Michael Church was established on 11th and Clinton Streets in 1849 and St. Bridget of Erin on Jefferson Avenue at Carr Street in 1853 to serve the Irish immigrants.

The location of the Irish churches and all the various descriptions of Kerry Patch lead to one conclusion, during the late 19th century Polish and Irish settlement areas overlapped.

In this setting, with great ceremony, the Poles laid the cornerstone for their new church on Sunday, July 16, 1882. The name of their parish honored the 16th century Polish saint, Stanislaus Kostka. Determined to become a Jesuit and despite the wishes of his influential father, Stanislaus walked 350 miles to enter the Jesuit order. He died at age 18, while a Jesuit seminarian.

The cornerstone ceremony for the original St. Stanislaus Church stirred nationalistic pride, and donations. Only three days later the building fund reached over $10,000. A mere four months passed before the new church was dedicated on Sunday, November 12, 1882 — with such festivities that everybody on the near north side of the City knew about it.

The ceremonies began with a procession or parade beginning near 18th Street and Washington Avenue.

"… a band and the thirty-six Knights of St. Wenceslaus… a fine body of men, well drilled, wearing plumes and baldrics of red and white," headed the procession.

Parts of the *Globe-Democrat's* description of the parade read like an article on fashion. "Then followed the fifty-one members of the St. Aloysius Society, with blue-colored and silvered-edged fringed sashes, marching to the music of a band. They, like the others, were Bohemians, and so was the next delegation of 200 men of the St. Wenceslaus Beneficial Society. They were excellently uniformed. Next came the Bohemian Roman Catholic Society of St. Joseph, 70 men, St. John Nepomuk's Bohemian

Society, 200, St. Stanislaus Society, only two months old, but with a membership of 130," the *Globe-Democrat* reported.

The parade marched through the neighborhoods north to Visitation Convent on Cass Avenue. There the priests and dignitaries joined the procession and marched to the new Polish church.

"Two Bishops and a number of clergymen were in attendance and over a thousand men belonging to societies, in regalia, headed by bands, and with flying flags and banners, participated in the procession, and lent dignity and grace to the occasion."

Bishop Ryan dedicated the church with, "Psalm and prayer, the sprinkling of the walls with holy water and their fuming with incense, were sung, said or performed according to the prescribed ritual."

Then the immense crowd in attendance surged into the church. Since pews had yet to be installed, standing room accommodated the huge numbers. Once again the reporter covered the dedication as if the article would appear in the style section of a modern newspaper. "The interior is very plain as yet. The 'stations of the cross,' pictures of the Sacred Hearts of Jesus and Mary, and a few others are the only adornment. Back of the

altar, however, the wall was very tastefully hung with greenery, and the altar was well lighted up and loaded with plants and flowers."

High mass was celebrated with a well-trained choir of young people furnishing the music. A bishop spoke to the crowd in English, another bishop delivered an address in German and a priest preached in Polish. Though the reporter didn't know what the priest said, he witnessed, "tears … on the cheeks of so many of the older members of the congregation."

The reporter was impressed at the ability of this small Polish community, with limited resources, to build their own church. He wrote, "Three years ago the Poles organized a congregation in St. Joseph's Church, since

▼ The original St. Stanislaus Parish church and school building as it appeared when it was dedicated in 1882.

23

then they have worshipped in the basement of St. Patrick's School, and though comparatively few and poor in the world's goods, they have collected, not outside of their own ranks, fully $9,000. It is but a short time since the cornerstone was laid with appropriate religious service, and now the $13,000 building, plain but substantial, is complete — seventy-five feet front, with schoolrooms on the first floor, church room above, ample cellarage, and residence for the priest."

The reporter also noted that, "There is very little debt upon it, and they have also 225 feet of ground available for future purposes."

The reporter described proposals among this small Polish community to build their own neighborhood. "As they are very frugal and saving, it is proposed by some of their friends to establish a building association which will purchase tracts of land in the neighborhood of the church, build on them and sell land and dwellings on easy terms to the people."

Gradually the church was decorated, and a parish library established.

In 1885, Father Urban Stanowski was appointed pastor. This Polish-American priest would demonstrate vision and management skills. He was able to foster both Roman Catholicism and Polish nationalism.

When he assumed pastorship, the parish had a debt of over $12,000. With his remarkable skills as an administrator, the entire debt was liquidated in three years. The total parish income for the three years was $15,828.55.

The parish purchased lots adjacent to the church in 1886. The following year, construction of a rectory, costing $6,000, began on those lots.

Brick townhouses, storefronts, rowhouses, apartments and flats were popping up on the vacant lots around St. Stanislaus. The surviving building permits record that Germans, Irish and some Poles were building homes.

Stanislaus Zebrowitz and C. Polinski built two story brick homes and tenements close to the Church. Michael Berner built a series of brick flats facing the church. Another neighbor built an addition to his home and added a then-fashionable mansard roof.

More high density development — apartments, stores and two story brick homes — continued to be built on nearby Cass Avenue in the late 1880's. John T. Flynn, who operated a grocery on Wash Street, built two story brick tenements on Cass, probably as investment property.

Just west of St. Stanislaus on 21st Street, two story brick rowhouses, apartments and storefronts were constructed in the mid and late 1880's. The names on the permits for these buildings were John Shannahan, Michael Bernal, Mary E. Page and a thoroughly mutilated interpretation of a Polish name, "Andrew Montkwoki."

While construction was booming around St. Stanislaus Church, the Olszewski Family was living at 1231 North 10th Street. The wage earners in the family were working as laborers, two of them in a broom factory.

One of the Poles from an earlier wave of immigrants, Julius Trojanowski, was opening doors to a new profession for the Poles. The St. Louis Police Board appointed Trojanowski to the department with the official rank of "Emergency Special" on November 23, 1887. The Police Board's annual report stated that 32 year-old Trojanowski was married, and his most recent employment had been as a grocer. The birthplace of each new recruit was listed, and Trojanowski was the only native born Pole appointed to the force, serving with many American-born and Irish-born officers. Only a year later, he was promoted to the rank of patrolman.

Many more recent immigrants from Poland were finding work in the mills along the river just north of Downtown. They settled into apartments nearby. Some settled in the far southeastern part of the city, called Carondelet, where foundries lined the river. Others found jobs and rooms in boarding houses in Frenchtown, later known as the Soulard and Kosciusko neighborhoods.

A committee of Polish immigrants wrote a letter dated July 24, 1889, that documents booming growth in the Polish community in the late 1880's. The letter is in a clear, beautiful script. Its grammatical errors reflect that the committee was writing in, what was for them, a foreign language. Their letter requested that the St. Louis Archdiocese establish a second Polish Parish, since the community had outgrown St. Stanislaus. They estimated the Polish Catholic community at approximately 3,000 people.

They wrote that St. Stanislaus Church was not large enough, "to accommodate one half of our people." They explained, "one Polish Priest, … , can not minister to the religious wants of three thousand people, which is about fair estimate of our countrymen in St. Louis." Committee members lamented that the children could not attend the parish school.

"We have pledges of over 300 hundred heads of families, (not belonging to the present parish for the lack of accommodation) who are willing and ready to contribute money enough for the support of Polish Priest in the new parish and the erection of another Polish Church."

The letter described another reason to establish a second Polish parish. The immigrants settling in the far northeastern end of the City and in the Carondelet neighborhood at the south end of the City needed three fares to take the streetcar to St. Stanislaus Church on 20th Street, "which is too expensive for poor and laboring people."

The committee found a building that would be more convenient to streetcar lines. They paid $5,000 for the former North St. Louis Church, a Protestant church that had stood on the corner of Mound and 8th Streets for decades. It was close to Broadway and its streetcar line, that stretched the entire length of the industrialized riverfront. This site would enable many immigrants in far North and in South City to take only one streetcar to church.

The ground floor of the old Protestant Church became the home of the new St. Casimir Parish Grade School, and the upper floor was the first home of St. Casimir Church. This second Polish parish was named in honor of the 15th century Polish prince who led an aesthectic life. The assistant pastor at St. Stanislaus was assigned to help establish St. Casimir Parish.

The harsh life and poverty afflicting the new immigrants is reflected in parish records. The first Baptism, on October 20, 1889, was followed only a week later by the first funeral. That funeral was conducted not for an elderly parishioner, but for Peter Szlag, only 1 and $\frac{1}{2}$ years-old.

According to the 1890 federal census, Polish-born St. Louisans numbered only 875, far fewer than the immigrant committee estimated a year earlier. The census figure, however, did not include the children of immigrants. And there may have been more Poles who were counted as the Russians, Austrians or Germans, who ruled their homeland.

In larger, more established Polish communities in the Eastern United States and in Chicago, fierce disputes were erupting between Polish immigrants and the Catholic church hierarchy. Controversy over the need for Polish priests for confessions and sermons and over the ownership of church property led to an open split in many congregations. Eventually, the controversies became hostile, and even led to separation from the Roman Catholic Church.

Perhaps the tension between Poles and the Catholic Church in the East made St. Louis Archbishop Peter Richard Kenrick more receptive to giving the local Poles a degree of independence. And the pastor of St. Stanislaus, Urban Stanowski, possessed an ability to cultivate the nationalistic and ethnic identity of his parishioners while nurturing good relations with the church hierarchy. In this atmosphere, with these parties involved, the government and responsibilities of caring for St. Stanislaus Parish were changed.

With the advice and consent of the Archbishop of St. Louis, on May 2, 1891, the parish was made a corporation in the State of Missouri. The legal name of the civil corporation, which would hold the title to the parish property, was the "Polish Roman Catholic St. Stanislaus Kostka Parish."

Father Stanowski remained under the jurisdiction of the Archbishop, while serving as the first president and treasurer of the corporation. The new board of trustees — Father Stanowski, Joseph Olszewski, John Grabowski, Joseph Grabowski, Michael Werozynski and Wladislaw Pilinski — held their first board meeting on May 6, 1891.

The first challenge was to meet the space needs of the growing Polish community. The congregation now numbered over 400 families plus many single adults. Perhaps their sense of ownership of their parish enabled this relatively small group of people — mostly recent immigrants, many of whom worked as laborers or factory workers making minimal pay — to build an extraordinary church.

Twenty thousand people attended the laying of the cornerstone of the new St. Stanislaus Church, on Sunday, September 13, 1891. The whole neighborhood was decorated for the festivities.

"The buildings in the neighborhood were profusely decorated with papal, Polish and American designs. Festoons of red, white and blue, alternating with the colors of Poland, were stretched across the streets. The adjacent street-space was packed solidly with people, and hundreds were compelled to watch the exercises at a distance without being able to hear what was going on," the *Globe-Democrat* reported the following morning.

Over 20 societies — Irish, German, Bohemian — each accompanied by a brass band, marched in the procession or parade along Cass Avenue to the building site.

"The children of the parish school occupied places on the platform and presented a very beautiful appearance," the *Globe-Democrat* reporter wrote.

Vicar General Muhlsiepen began the ceremonies with an address in German, and was followed by an address in the Polish language by Father Urban Stanowski. Then, "Muhlsiepen took the trowel and spread the mortar. The stone was then lowered to its place, and the foundation of one the of the largest Polish Roman Catholic churches in the West was laid."

Among those who attended the ceremonies was Polish-American Peter Kiolbassa, the City Treasurer of Chicago, and his family.

Stanowski seems to have influenced the concept of the design of the new church. The architects who carried out that concept were two German immigrants — Louis Wessbecher and Charles Hummel, who had recently formed the firm of Wessbecher & Hummel. At the time they designed the new St. Stanislaus, Hummel was about 35 years old. He had emigrated to the United States in 1879. Wessbecher was about 33 years old and had studied at the Polyclinic of Karlsruhe and the Institute of Stuttgart. He emigrated to the United States in 1883, and married the Missouri-born daughter of German immigrants, Anna.

The church they designed cost about $92,000 to build and its construction required about a year. The results wowed St. Louis.

▲ This image from a marriage certificate shows the original murals, sanctuary and windows of St. Stanislaus church. The interior decoration was altered after the fire of 1928. (Document courtesy of Donna and John Nachefski.)

The church was called Roman-Polish, or Byzantine-Romanesque. Its mix of styles must have seemed exotic to its Irish and German neighbors.

The church's great dome, sheathed in shimmering copper, towered over the neighborhood. At a height of 175 feet, the dome rose 15 feet higher than the dome of the Old Courthouse. The *Globe-Democrat* reported that the dome was, "flanked on either side by towers 150 feet high." The dimensions of the church were 90 feet by 145 feet. The door and window openings formed Romanesque arches. Subtle designs in the red brick created patterns across the facade of the church.

St. Stanislaus Kostka, unique in its city, had a seating capacity of 1,300. The building itself, one of the largest church buildings in the city, was a physical statement of the Polish presence in St. Louis.

The interior provided another exceptional experience. Arched windows circling the base of the dome showered light into the core of the church. The *Globe-Democrat* described the effect. "The interior of the church needed no bunting, flags or evergreen to add to its beauty. The large and spacious dome admitted the bright rays of the sun, giving the interior a bright golden tinge."

The dedication of this completed church, on Sunday, September 18, 1892, was the cause for another neighborhood celebration. "Sometime before the services began the people of that vicinity were out decorating the house-tops and the church," according to the *Globe-Democrat*. "The neighborhood presented a very pretty appearance with gay colored bunting spanning the street from portico to portico, and the national flags of Poland and America floating in the breeze from the fences and each corner of the church while the fence in front was profusely decorated with cedar and evergreen."

A choir of forty-five voices, accompanied by a twelve-piece band, chanted Gounod's High Mass. There were "discourses" in German, English and Polish. The four-hour-long dedication service was attended by a large delegation from Chicago.

After the new church was dedicated, the area around St. Stanislaus Church continued to develop. August Hauschild, who lived on Cass near the church, built four adjacent three story brick storefronts and flats on Cass in 1892. Two years later he built three more adjacent two story brick flats.

A new feature would be added to St. Stanislaus Church in 1893. Father Stanowski returned to Poland during that summer. His attempt to pray at the most hallowed religious shrine in Poland, Jasna Gora in Czestochowa, was thwarted. He had been blacklisted by the Russian occupying authorities. During the trip, however, he obtained a late 18th century replica of the icon of the Black Madonna of Czestochowa, and its marble altar, from a monastery in Cracow. At that time, it was believed to be one of only two copies of this symbol of Polish nationalism and religious freedom. He placed the replica in St. Stanislaus Church.

During the fall semester of 1893, 25 boys and 35 girls were attending St. Casimir School. One teacher, Mr. Budo, taught all 60 children. Mr. Budo was obviously accustomed to large numbers of children. He and his wife Josephine had emigrated with their eldest son in 1880 from Poland. After settling in Missouri, they had eight more children. Directories and census records list Budo as a laborer and as an organist at various times. He likely pursued all these trades to support his growing family in his new country.

At St. Stanislaus, Father Stanowski officiated at the wedding of Michael Olszewski to Polish-born Antonina. Their first child, Stella, was born in 1894. In his thirties, Olszewski was pursuing a career as a glazier.

A handwritten census of Polish immigrants dating to early or mid 1890's recorded where numbers of Polish families were living. Twenty-one Polish households were shown living in Frenchtown, or Soulard. Fifteen Polish families were recorded as living in Carondelet.

The census was coded to indicate the families attending St. Stanislaus, St. Casimir, other parishes or "not attending any church."

It documents large numbers of Poles living on the Near North Side, near the industries.

Eleven families were listed with addresses on Main, two Polish households on 6th Street, eight on 7th Street, two dozen on 8th Street, 30 on 9th Street, eleven families on 10th Street, five on 11th Street, two dozen on 12th Street, five households on 13th Street, 23 families on 14th Street, and eight on Mound Street.

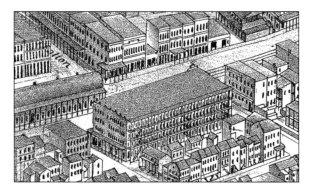

▲ The four story Ashley Building at O'Fallon Street and North Broadway served as a port of entry for waves of new Polish imigrants to St. Louis. Compton & Dry's drawing depicts the market building on North Broadway, adjacent to the tenement.

One building, the Ashley Building at 1242 N. Broadway, was listed separately. This four-story tenement had slowly evolved from an Irish tenement building, to housing so many recent immigrants from Poland, that it was called "The Polish Capitol." Forty-nine Polish households were identified as living in this building in this census.

Railroad tracks, the St. Louis Grain Elevator, a huge sugar refinery, a pork house and a belt factory dominated the blocks between the Mississippi River and the Ashley Building. Major iron works were located to the South. Across Broadway stood the old City Market, built in 1857.

New immigrants were lengthening the rolls of nearby St. Casimir parish. This spurred the congregation to buy land adjacent to their church, at 8th and Mullanphy Streets, to build a larger church. In July of 1895, the cornerstone for the new church building was laid. Wessbecher & Hummel, the architects of St. Stanislaus Church, designed this combination school and church building. The following October, the new church was dedicated.

Though the challenges of adapting to a new nation, city, language and jobs consumed tremendous time and energy, the Poles did not forget their heritage. In May of 1895, the Polish people of St. Louis draped St. Stanislaus Church in mourning in commemoration of the 100th anniversary of the partition of Poland. A century earlier, the democratic spirit in Poland, inspired by the American constitution, had threatened the despots of Europe. So the

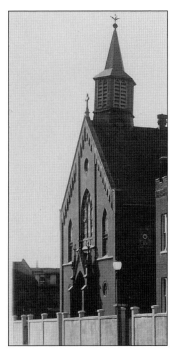

▲ The facade of the second St. Casimir Parish Church building, which was dedicated in 1895. (Photo courtesy of Linda Lawson.)

Austrian, German and Russian empires chopped up Poland, dismantled it as a nation, and wiped it off the map. In mourning for the century of oppression of their native Poland, the Polish people of St. Stanislaus made resolutions to abstain from entertainment.

While propagating their Polish heritage, the parishioners were assimilating. In 1896, St. Stanislaus Parish began offering English classes in the evening.

St. Stanislaus numbered 2,300 parishioners. Franciscan Sisters of Olenburg taught 450 children in the parish school and 945 parishioners participated in one or more of the seven parish societies.

While the number of Poles in St. Stanislaus Parish was growing, the number of Poles living in the south end of the Soulard neighborhood, then known as Frenchtown, was growing too. In 1896, they united to form a brotherhood named the Society of Tadeusz Kosciusko, in honor of the Polish patriot who fought with the American colonial army in the Revolutionary War.

The following year, Polish-American Julius Trojanowski achieved a personal goal, that was also a first for his community. The St. Louis Police Department promoted Trojanowski from a patrolman to a sergeant.

Despite there being a more established Polish community, that could ease the transition for immigrants, the new arrivals from Poland faced hardships and callousness.

The story of young Agnes Flowers reflects that crushing harshness.

Agnes Flowers turned 15 on April 14, 1897. Her family sometimes used their Polish name, Kwiatkowska, and sometimes its English translation, Flowers. Agnes lived with her family at 1325 N. 20th Street, only a block from St. Stanislaus Koskta Church. She was described as, "a child in years," but, "a woman in strength and size. She was handsome, tall and well built, with light colored and luxuriant hair, large blue eyes, a clear, pink complexion and a happy disposition."

When her father lost his job, she found a job working in the finishing department of a shoe factory. Her meager salary from Friedman Bros. & Schafer shoe factory at 3417 Locust Street was supporting her parents and three younger siblings.

Saturday, February 20, 1898, young Agnes Flowers was at work on the second floor of the shoe factory on Locust Street in Midtown St. Louis.

Young Agnes was standing near, perhaps leaning on, the grate of the elevator shaft when the platform was descending from the fifth floor. The day before, a new elevator boy had been hired. Whether or not anyone needed the elevator to stop, the automatic gates raised every time a floor was passed, leaving the shaft open.

The *Post-Dispatch* reported that the gate lifted before the car was, "level with the floor. The gate struck her (Agnes) on the back of the head and stunned her."

Agnes tumbled down a forty-foot shaft and, "gave one agonizing shriek as she plunged, …"

"Half a hundred girls who worked with her heard the cry and saw the frightful plunge, but were powerless to assist her."

Her brother-in-law and fellow factory worker, Tony Schultz, ran down the stairs and was the first to get to her. The *Post-Dispatch* described the pitiful scene. "He reached under the car and caught her maimed and broken body in his strong arms and bore her upstairs.

She was limp and her eyes were closed. She did not utter a word, and a shudder convulsed her body."

She was rushed to City Hospital. Her skull, nose and both arms and legs were fractured. There were more internal injuries. The physicians did not expect her to survive.

A *Post-Dispatch* reporter called the factory. "The man in the office, told the reporter he did not know the name of the injured girl, nor where she lived. He said she was not much hurt and that he and all the other employees were too busy to make further investigation."

On Sunday her father insisted upon taking Agnes home, where she died.

While most of the Poles were struggling to make their way in their new nation, building permits reflect that some were achieving enough financial security to build new homes near St. Stanislaus. August Piluski built a two story brick home near the church in 1897, and Valentine Grodski, a bricklayer by profession, built a home at the north end of the block.

The doorway into St. Louis for many of the new Polish immigrants continued to be the Ashley Building. This tenement was featured in an article in the St. Louis Republic on July 23, 1898.

The four-story building was described as rectangular, with a flat roof, similar to a barracks, "with a dark, dismal cellar under the whole." There were 248 rooms, including the 12 storerooms on the ground floor. "Last winter the census showed in the neighborhood of 600 souls quartered there," the paper reported.

The paper presented an ominous description of the crowded tenement. "The boarded windows, the broken stairways, the battered cornices and the shattered window panes give it the appearance of a battle-scarred reminder of civil strife … in the rear it looks as though its walls had been pierced by a thousand canon," the article stated. "Each of the four stories of the building are plainly marked by broad porches extending entirely across the rear, the roof of the one below forming the floor of its more elevated companion… Narrow wooden stairways connect with the bottom floor. Many of the supports have been displaced and thrown out of line until the whole structure seems to be momentarily threatening to topple over… The ends of the building are walls of solid masonry, pierced by only a few scattering windows." It appeared as, "an abandoned fortress."

At that time, "Over ninety percent of the tenants are Polanders and the remaining ten percent is made up of Hungarians, Slavs and Swedes, with an occasional Celt to vary the monotony," the article stated. "Time was when the Irish held sway in the Ashley Building, but the plodding and persistent Polanders have gradually supplanted them."

Conservative estimates of the number of Poles who came and went through the portals of Ashley was 10,000.

Neighborhoods

By the turn of the 20th century, St. Louis was the fourth largest city in the United States with a population of 575,000 residents. Within its 61 square miles, the commonfields had been transformed into busy warehouse and factory districts, a Downtown filled with new skyscrapers, and bustling neighborhoods.

Its dynamic population included communities from Ireland, Bavaria, Prussia, Alsace-Loraine, Bohemia, … Newer and growing communities of Italians, Serbians, Russians, Lebanese, and Ruthenians were building homes, churches, businesses and neighborhoods.

In this remarkable setting Polish immigrants were fueling St. Louis' industries with their muscle, establishing small businesses, forming fraternal, social and cultural associations, and creating distinctive communities that would enhance the texture and character of St. Louis.

By 1900, St. Louis' Polish community included at least 2,535 residents whose birthplace was Poland. According to the 1900 census, 1,248 of the St. Louis Poles were from Russian-occupied or eastern Poland. Ninety-five census entries did not specify a region of Poland. The compendium for the census included 1,192 St. Louisans from German-occupied Poland.

The new St. Louis Poles along with second and third generation Poles had developed two ethnic neighborhoods and operated two active, substantial parishes.

The immediate neighborhood of St. Stanislaus Kostka Church had evolved into a Polish community by the turn of the century. The census entries for the 1400 block of North 20th Street, for example, document that the block was crowded with Polish families. These families were overwhelmingly from western

Poland, which was ruled by Germany. The block also seemed to be home to the more well-established Polish families, rather than the new arrivals from Poland.

In addition to being the site of the entire parish complex, the 1400 block of North 20th was home to over 70 Polish households. Only a handful of these families came from eastern Poland, which was occupied by the Russians. About ten Irish families, eight German families, an English family, a French-Canadian family and two families from France also called the block home.

Though many of the entries are blurred and discolored with time, leaving them hard to decipher, the census still presents a clear image of the density of the neighborhood. Many of the census entries document that the family unit included adult brothers and sisters, or adult children. The number of Polish adults who called the block home was over 150. Over 200 Polish American children lived on the same block.

Three of the Polish Americans had emigrated in the 1860's, at least 30 had emigrated in the 1870's, more than 70 had emigrated in the 1880's, and about 50 were recent immigrants, arriving in the United States in the 1890's.

These Polish Americans powered St. Louis' new manufacturing economy.

The 1900 U.S. census documented that at least 17 Polish residents of the block worked in St. Louis' huge tobacco processing industry. About two dozen residents worked in the shoe industry. One Pole worked in a frame factory, and one was a wood turner.

The industrializing of St. Louis was reflected in the number of wage earners who were making things. The residents included a box maker, a broom maker, a cabinet maker, eight chair makers, one furniture maker, a wagon maker, a vinegar maker, a gas maker, tailors and shirt makers. Polish residents of the block also worked, in rolling mills, as shop foremen, and as a machine hand. One Pole on the block became a "stove moulder" in the city's tremendous industry producing first coal stoves and later the new gas stoves.

Two teamsters and one carriage driver lived on the block.

A few of the Poles on the block were moving into the construction trades. Block residents included a bricklayer and an apprentice electrician.

The path into small business in many immigrant communities began with opening a corner saloon — and one Pole on the block was a saloon keeper. There was also a Polish American insurance agent and a bookkeeper, a letter carrier, a waiter, a housekeeper, and a janitor living on the church block. The census described at least 30 wage earners on the block as "laborers."

Innovative Father Stanowski found new ways to encourage the growth of St. Stanislaus Parish in this developing Polish-American community. In 1901, he helped Franciscan sisters form their own order — the Franciscan Sisters of Our Lady of Perpetual Help — with their mother house located in the parish. The order started with three Polish sisters.

To help the community keep its ethnic music traditions, new Polish hymnals were purchased for the parishioners.

The parish was making continual, small improvements to their complex — a brick wall bordering the property, a frame shelter, alterations to the buildings. One building permit suggests that St. Stanislaus Parish had one of the most elaborate outhouses on the Near North Side of St. Louis. The City issued a permit in 1902 for a one story

▲ On their first date, Teofil and Teofilia Chrostowski visited the 1904 World's Fair. This photo was taken on their wedding day, May 30, 1905. (Photo courtesy of Linda Lawson.)

brick addition to the out house. The addition was estimated to cost the then substantial sum of $700.

During the first years of the 20th century, more of the Polish neighbors and members of St. Stanislaus Parish were not just living in the area, but becoming homeowners. Building permits, which list the property owners, reflect this trend. The City clerks struggled to understand yet spell the Polish names of homeowners. They issued permits to construct, renovate or make additions to homes or businesses to J. Kossewski, J. Swientkoski, A. Gusinsky, John Pokoiski, E. Zebrowski, W. Waurzyniak, Saranfinski, F. Hazrelewski, J. L. Screwsgewske, Wal Grodzki,… When the same name appeared on several permits, the spellings often changed each time the Polish name was written.

Though the immediate parish neighborhood had become a Polish community, the building permit records reveal that their Irish neighbors continued to own and build on the block. The Irish names Timothy Driscoll, John O'Malley, John Barry and James Sheridan appear on permits for the neighborhood at the beginning of the 20th century.

These building permits suggest that the Polish Americans and Irish Americans were successfully and happily living together.

With the growth in numbers, businesses, financial resources, and sense of community, the Poles were ready to establish more social and cultural institutions. By 1906, the Polish American Hall Association had purchased and cleared property on Cass Avenue, around the corner from St. Stanislaus Church. In August of that year, the Poles began construction of a one and one-half story, brick hall, estimated to cost $30,000. Local Polish societies contributed funds to build and maintain the hall, known as Dom Polski. A board of directors managed it as a commercial enterprise, which evolved into a social center for the Polish community.

The St. Louis chapter or Nest #45 of the Polish Falcons had formed in 1905. The motto of this fraternal organization, which originated in Poland in 1867, was "a healthy spirit in a healthy body." Similar to the German Turnvereins and Bohemian Sokols, the Falcons fostered physical fitness, intellectual exercise, and a rich cultural life. In the United States, these organizations encouraged political and civic involvement that respected their homelands while celebrating American citizenship. The St. Louis Nest held its first gym classes at the Stolles Hall at 13th and Biddle Streets. In 1907, the Falcons took part in the dedication of the new Polish Hall on Cass Avenue. Soon their gymnastics and calisthenics classes and drills were conducted in the newly completed Polish Hall. As the Falcons raised funds, they bought equipment and they expanded their gymnastics to exercises on the double bars, horizontal bar, horse and rings.

August Marchlewski, who lived at 4747 Nebraska Avenue in far South City, demonstrated his determination to start another Polish Parish. A fireman by profession, Marchlewski mortgaged his home for $1,700. He used the money to buy property in his Mount Pleasant neighborhood, in the southeastern quadrant of the City, as a site for a new Polish community and a parish complex. Then he approached Father Victor Stepka to help establish a Polish Parish.

While most of the Polish immigrants lived in crowded neighborhoods, near heavy industry and near the river, the Mount Pleasant neighborhood consisted of open fields and truck farms. Just to the north was the busy, old settlement of St. Anthony or "the Monk's" Church, a German Parish. Stringtown Road, an early road renamed Virginia Avenue, formed the western boundary of the neighborhood. To the east was the string of development along South

▲ This home-made chapel in the basement of the flat at 4747 Nebraska Avenue in the Mount Pleasant neighborhood was the first home of St. Hedwig Parish.

Broadway and the Mississippi. To the south was Carondelet, with its industry.

Though framed by the 18th and 19th century settlements, Mount Pleasant itself remained small farms with only scattered houses. Here Polish families could afford to buy lots and build homes.

When he arrived in the neighborhood, Reverend Victor Stepka found that August Marchlewski and Joseph Wisniewski, an iron worker who lived close to St. Stanislaus, had already brought together twelve families ready to organize a parish. The twelve included shoe repairmen William Doetzel, John Kwiatkowski, and tinsmith John Pytlinski, who all lived in or near the Mount Pleasant neighborhood.

On June 5, 1904, the first mass of the new parish was celebrated in a temporary chapel created in the basement of Marchlewski's flat on Nebraska Avenue. The parish was named in honor of St. Hedwig, the 12th and 13th century Queen of Silesia who founded monasteries and promoted Christianity.

An article titled, "Carondelet Priest sells building lots," described the "novel scheme" for having the "congregation close to the church." The article in the Carondelet News explained that the parish owned blocks of property facing Itaska Street and parts of adjacent blocks. This was the land Marchlewski had paid for by mortgaging his home. Except for the piece of property reserved for church buildings, the entire purchase was divided into lots and sold to future parishioners. The net profit of the lots paid for the property reserved for the parish buildings.

Twenty-four Polish families had purchased home sites on the church blocks by the time the article was published in the Carondelet News on September 10, 1904.

The blessing of the corner stone for the new church took place in October 1904. A parish souvenir booklet stated, "The blessing was performed by the Most Rev. Archbishop (John Glennon)," who mentioned that he can rely on the faith of the Polish people, and that

"St. Hedwig Parish started with twelve families as though with twelve Apostles."

According to the booklet published for the 25th anniversary of the parish, "entire groups of sodalities and societies marched to St. Hedwig's from North St. Louis…" "Nearly all the Polish sodalities and societies in the city were represented."

The parishioners planned to build their parish complex in stages. The architects of St. Stanislaus Church, Wessbecher & Hummel, designed a three-story combination church, rectory and school building for the south side Polish parish.

The city issued a permit for the first phase of the complex — the lower two stories of the combination church, school and rectory. The estimated cost of construction for the ground floor and first floor of the parish building was $13,950. The corners of the building were capped with decorative terra cotta finials, to give the building a more finished look until the upper floor could be built.

The ground floor was fashioned into classrooms and a residence for the priest while the first floor was used as a sanctuary. In the spring of 1905, the school opened with an enrollment of 46 children.

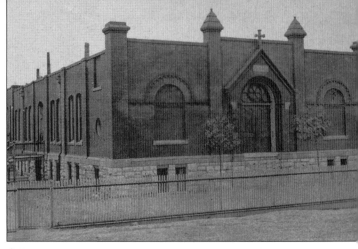

▲ St. Hedwig parishioners constructed their combination church and school building in phases. The ground floor and first floor of the building facing Pulaski Street at Compton Avenue were dedicated in 1905.

The new St. Hedwig Church faced Hiawatha Street, which was soon renamed Pulaski Street in honor of the Polish American hero who had been killed fighting for the colonists in the Revolutionary War. Poles began constructing homes around their new church. Some of the Polish names recorded on building permits for the area are similar to names on permits for construction around St. Stanislaus Parish. However, the Anglo or German clerks used such a variety of phonetic spellings for the Polish names, that some are distorted and disguised almost beyond recognition.

Shortly after the parish opened, John Kallinowski was issued a permit to build a single family home on one of the adjacent lots on Pulaski Street. The names Kiriotowsky, Sharafiniski, Joseph Wisnewski, A. Jurkiewigz, M. Kalmowski and John Burdozy appear on permits to build homes and flats on the church block. Some names appear to be on multiple permits, with a variety of spellings.

The neighborhood newspaper, the Carondelet News, reported that Michael Kolkowki purchased the ground and building at 4619 Michigan. On July 14, 1906, Casimir Staminski signed a contract to build a two story, four family flat at 4620-22 Virginia Avenue, near St. Hedwig. The cost of construction was estimated at $5,600.

The cost of constructing a one story, single family home ranged from $1,200 to $1,500, while the two story, two and four -families cost

$2,600 to $5,800 to build.

Reverend S.J. Zielinski was appointed pastor of St. Hedwig in February of 1906. That fall, 126 children started school there.

The parish trustees sold a lot with a 25-foot frontage opposite the church lots on Itaska to John Jastrzemski. The sale price was $2,495. Fifteen years earlier, John and Kate Jastrzemski had emigrated from German-occupied Poland, with their daughter Apolonia and sons Ladislaus and Bronislaus. John supported his family as a laborer in a glassworks. His sons would find employment as shoe workers.

Within a few years, brick homes and flats would line the streets around St. Hedwig Church.

With the Polish community developing, St. Hedwig's parishioners were able to complete their combination church and school building in 1907. The top floor cost $11,000 to build.

While the parish was expanding, and while the Poles were building homes, Pastor Zielinski was a crime victim. On Thursday night, August 1, 1906, a poultry thief entered the parish hen house on Pulaski Street. The thief absconded with three geese and two ducks, all valued at $1.00.

▼ The combination church and school building of St. Hedwig Parish after the upper floors were added, completing the building in 1907.

The numbers of Poles settling at the southern end of Soulard continued to increase as new immigrants found work at the American Car Foundry, known as the "Car Shop." The foundry, located in several shops east of Broadway near Anheuser-Busch, manufactured street cars, trucks and coaches for light rail. Hania Turek, a Polish St. Louisan from the Soulard area, recalled, "If asked where you live John, his answer would be 'car shop.' Where you eat John, likewise, he would answer 'car shop'. That was the extent of the immigrant's vocabulary."

Machine shop foreman Jozef Stygar, woodworker Tomasz Przybylski, grocer Adam Sadowski, laborer Tomasz Czasnochy, and saloon keeper Francis Reichert were among the members of a small committee formed to start a parish in Frenchtown. Committee members pooled their savings and raised $7,000. They purchased a vacant school building from the First German Evangelical Lutheran Trinity Congregation for $5,750 for the new Our Lady of Czestochowa Parish. They transformed the second floor into their church.

The first mass was celebrated Christmas Day in 1907. "Soon after, the school was built under the church with the help of a contractor named Baran and was assisted by the parishioners," according to Hania Turek, who recorded parishioners' and her own memories of the parish. The parish started with 50 families, and 47 students in the school.

While these two Polish Roman Catholic Parishes were forming in South St. Louis, a revolutionary new group came into being in North City.

A large group of Poles in North City belonged to an association named in honor of a Polish playwright, the Aleksander Fredro Literary Society. Many of these Poles were members of St. Casimir Parish, located at 8th and Mullanphy Streets. Their library received Polish periodicals from Chicago and the East Coast that were chronicling the birth of a new, Polish branch of Catholicism — the Polish National Catholic Church.

This denomination, begun in Scranton, Pennsylvania in the 1890's, resulted from disputes between Polish Catholic parishes and their Archdiocese over language and management of the parishes. The Polish Catholics wanted sermons in the Polish language and to be able to sing Polish hymns. The bishop agreed that if they built a new church, he would assign them a Polish priest and they could use their language and their traditional hymns. These Catholic Poles built churches. But the bishop did not respect the agreement.

The disenchanted Poles formed the Polish National Catholic Church. Mass was in their native tongue. Their ritual was Roman Catholic, but the responsibility for financial management of the parish was in the hands of the parishioners.

In St. Louis, members of the Aleksander Fredro Literary Society organized Sts. Cyril and Methodius Polish National Catholic Church in 1907. Their congregation was named for the ninth century brothers who served as missionaries to the Slavs. They purchased the old church at 2011 N. 11th Street, in the Old North St. Louis neighborhood. Local architect Eugene Greenleaf had designed the church building in 1857 for the North Presbyterian Church. The old Anglo Presbyterian church building, becoming the home of a new Polish congregation, reflected the ethnic evolution of the neighborhood.

The sanctuary filled the upper floor of the church building. The high ground floor served as a hall. The members of the new Sts. Cyril and Methodius Church built a stage in the ground floor.

A decree signed by Archbishop John Glennon, on March 14, 1908, excommunicated nine Polish St. Louisans and cautioned parishioners of St. Casimir Parish.

Found among family records of St. Casimir parishioners, the decree seems to have been in response to the establishment of Sts. Cyril and Methodius Polish National Catholic Church. It also substantiates that former members of St. Casimir helped establish the new Polish National Catholic Church.

The decree reads, "By these presents, we hereby declare that all those here mentioned, to-wit:- Ignacy Kubysiak, Michael Wozniak, Stephen K. Pruski, Wojciech Jedraszkiewiez, Jakob Baczyk, Stanislaw Wichlenski, Frank Jozwiak, John Krzeminski, Jakiob Konsiewicz, in so far as they have been members of the Roman Catholic Church are hereby declared to be by name excommunicated therefrom.

"They may not return to the Catholic Church until they have made due and ample apology for the part they have taken in creating and fostering a schismatic and protestant Church and until they give such other satisfaction as we deem in each case necessary.

"Further, we hereby declare that after this announcement all members of St. Casimir's Church who will attend services at a schismatic or protestant Church are by that act excommunicated and the absolution from this censure we reserve to ourselves."

With this decree, the Archbishop had excommunicated Polish immigrant laborers, machinists, and butchers. These Poles lived in rowhouses, tenements and alley houses on North 10th, 12th, and 13th Streets and on Cass Avenue.

The character of their neighborhood, and neighborhoods near or overlapping the Polish settlements around Sts. Cyril and Methodius, St. Casimir and St. Stanislaus was described in the Civic Plan for St. Louis, which was published in 1907. The plan detailed the crowded conditions in parts of the near north side.

The area bounded by Seventh Street on the east, Fourteenth Street on the west, Morgan Street on the south, and Cass Avenue on the north, was home to 21,762 St. Louisans. According to the civic plan, the average density per acre was 206.49 residents.

Civic leaders noted in the plan that two needs of the area were being addressed. Recently opened Patrick Henry School was equipped

◀ The wedding photo of Joseph and Mary Penski who were married in 1909 at St. Casimir Church. (Photo courtesy of Roger Krasnicki.)

with, "every modern educational device and adapted especially to the needs of the crowded population." And the first free municipal bath was under construction on Tenth Street between Cass Avenue and Biddle Street.

The text also referred to all the ethnic groups living in the general area. "The belt of negroes between Eleventh and Thirteenth Streets separate the two districts." The Carr Square neighborhood, "is becoming more and more densely populated, … The population of this district consisted formerly of Germans, Irish and Americans, but within the last five years there has been a large influx of Russian Jews. ….sweeping the Americans gradually westward to Jefferson Avenue, the Irish and Germans to the north, and the negoes to the south and immediately east of this district." The report continued to describe the St. Casimir Parish territory, stating, "Still further east are the Italians and the Poles."

Some Poles left the crowded neighborhoods of North City for the Mount Pleasant Neighborhood in South City, and the opportunity it offered to buy a one-family brick house at comparatively reasonable prices. By 1909, St. Hedwig Parish numbered 154 families, and the following year 169 families.

The political environment in Poland spurred young Poles like Aleksander Sutkowski to immigrate to the United States. At age 18, Sutkowski would automatically be drafted into the Army of the Russian Czar. Like many Polish teenagers determined to escape the Russian draft, Sutkowski fled Poland, arriving in St. Louis in 1910. Two years later he married Marta, also an immigrant, at the new Sts. Cyril and Methodius Church.

In 1910, Polish-born Julius L. Trojanowski was serving his adopted city as a Police Sergeant working in the City's Fourth District. Trojanowski, who lived with his family at 2945 Cass Avenue, received, "medals for meritorious and fine work." In addition he was the holder of one gold medal for, "the bravest act during one year, …" A Police Department publication stated that, "He is a Polish officer and his countrymen as well as the native citizens respect him. The Sergeant is known as a good organizer and his men have to toe the mark."

Another Pole was becoming an artistic entrepreneur in St. Louis. Michael Olszewski left the studios of stained glass artist Emil Frei to open his own art and stained glass studio. He built a storefront with an apartment on the second floor at 4644 Virginia Avenue, near St. Hedwig Parish, to serve as his studio and home.

After 1900, new immigrants were building a growing community in the Frenchtown and Soulard area of South St. Louis. Unlike the new Polish community in Mount Pleasant, where the Poles settled for the opportunity to build homes, jobs attracted the Poles to Frenchtown. The oldest part of Frenchtown, east of Broadway, not only provided new immigrants entry level jobs in heavy industry, but less expensive housing near the industry.

Polish immigrant Frank Rau, who had donated one of the stained glass windows for Our Lady of Czestochowa Church, lived on the 1200 block of South Third Street in Frenchtown. His block, for example, had a substantial and growing settlement of Polish immigrants by the time of the 1910 census. Rau headed one of the most established Polish households on the block. The 45 year-old had migrated in 1898, and worked in an Irish dominated profession. He was a "trucker" at the nearby freight depot.

Rau's 32 year-old wife, Marie, had emigrated in 1900. Both Frank and Marie were able to speak English. The Raus had three children, their five year old son born in Pennsylvania, and one year-old and four year-old daughters born in Missouri. To add to their income, Marie had three boarders living in their home. The three boarders, who like the Raus came from the part of Poland occupied by Russia, worked as laborers in the freight depot and soap factory.

The Raus' neighborhood would have been a hard place to learn, sometimes even hear, English. The Federal Census of 1910 shows that the 1200 block of South Third Street was an amalgam of Eastern Europeans, with only a handful of residents of Irish, Scottish, or English descent.

The crowded block, with housing packed between commerce, was home to 64 households. Over half of the households, 36, were Polish.

Twenty-two of the Polish households had emigrated from the part of their homeland occupied by the Austrian Empire, and twelve from the part dominated by the Russian Empire.

The block was a neighborhood of overwhelmingly new immigrants, trying to get established in jobs and communities in their chosen country. Only two adult Polish residents were American-born. A mere three of the 98 Polish, adult residents had emigrated in the 1880's. Only eleven Poles had emigrated in the 1890's. The great majority of individual Poles had emigrated between 1900 and 1910, with the greatest number, 21, immigrating to the United States the previous year, 1909.

Unlike the Bohemian immigrants, who emigrated as families, these Polish St. Louisans appear to have emigrated as young, single adults, or as young married people. That is evidenced by the fact that almost all the children in the Polish households were born in the United States.

The Poles on the 1200 block of South 3rd Street were employed in demanding, physical work. There was a carpenter, a house painter, a trucker, two coal miners, two iron workers, a concrete mixer, two meat packers, and one young Polish lady worked as a packer in a bakery.

The census described the great majority of the Poles as laborers. Fifteen of the laborers found work in soap factories. Probably most of them worked at N.K. Fairbank soap manufacturer, which was located on the next block at 1114 South 3rd Street, though some of them may have worked at the other neighborhood soap factory, Schaeffer Bros & Powell Mfg. Co. at 2401 Kosciusko Street. The census documented six Polish laborers working in a "car shop," which would have been the American Car Foundry at Russell Boulevard and DeKalb. Six worked in a tobacco factory, seven in railroad yards, and seven in a freight depot. Another major employer of the Poles, employing both men and women, was the rope and burlap bag factory. Poles worked as weavers and laborers.

Bemis Brothers Bag Company, located in the neighborhood at 601 S. 4th Street, produced all kinds of bags and imported burlap. Several Poles worked as laborers and firemen at the nearby gas plant. Three more Poles worked as firemen at a local stationary plant.

Many of the Polish women developed a home-based business supported by the new immigrants. Sixteen Polish households took in boarders or lodgers.

The lady of the house cooked, cleaned and often did the laundry for their boarders. The Polish ladies of the 1200 block of South Third Street provided food and lodging for at least 34 Polish immigrants. All but two of the boarders were men. The boarding houses provided a stepping stone in emigration between the Polish home town and St. Louis. The emigrants from Russian-ruled Poland boarded with families also from Russian-occupied Poland. And the households that had emigrated from Austrian-ruled Poland took in boarders from Austrian-ruled Poland.

Most of the neighbors of the Poles on South Third Street were emigrants from Slovakia, Russia, Slovenia, or of German ancestry. One couple described themselves as,

Russian "Yiddish." Like the Poles, some of these households took in boarders, increasing the number of working adults residing on the street. There were a few second generation German-American residents, who probably helped with the transition into American society and the economy.

A handful of Swiss, Armenian, Greek, Bohemian and Roumanian born Americans also called the block home.

This eastern part of Frenchtown, which was a port of entry for Polish immigrants, gradually transformed into a Polish neighborhood — thanks to the growing spiritual and community life around Our Lady of Czestochowa Parish.

The development of the Polish community around St. Stanislaus also had been evolving for almost 30 years. A book published in 1911, *Notable Catholic Institutions of St. Louis and Vicinity*, made a little slur at the Irish while complimenting the Poles of St. Stanislaus. It stated, "What was formerly the very heart of 'Kerry Patch' has been transformed into a most respectable neighborhood."

A small business community was developing to serve the Polish-Americans on the North Side. The Polish Publishing Co., which published St. Louis' Polish weekly, Louis Dombkiewicz's barber shop, Michael Kaszewski's saloon, and John Streszewski's cigar shop operated on Cass Avenue near the Polish Hall. On 20th Street near the church, Julian Pilinski taught music and Anna Jablonski made dresses. Their neighbor Johanna Kulinska delivered babies. Michael Mantkowski operated a grocery store across the alley from the church, on 21st Street. The Polish Hall also maintained a Polish language library.

The Polish Financial Association was

chartered as a Corporation in the State of Missouri in 1912. This building and loan association originated in 1907 and met with great success. The institution, which operated as a bank, had offices on the first floor of the Polish Hall.

In 1912, the skyline of the Polish neighborhood on 20th Street changed. A leak in the roof of St. Stanislaus church was damaging the beautifully painted and stenciled interior domes of the church. It was determined that the only way to effectively and efficiently stop the leak was to remove the copper-sheathed dome of the church. The loss of the dome, that dominated and defined the neighborhood skyline, was regretted, even grieved.

At the same time, a small Polish community evolving in the Walnut Park neighborhood of North City established St. Adalbert Parish, named for the patron saint of Poland. At first they held services in the Chapel of St. Mary's Orphanage, which had opened in Walnut Park at

▶ Anufry Liszewski kept this post card of the ship that brought him to his new homeland in 1913. His name was originally "Lis." He was advised that entrance into the United States was more difficult for Jews and that his name sounded Jewish. To improve his chances of being allowed into the United States, the Polish immigrant changed his last name from "Lis" to "Liszewski." (Document courtesy of John and Philip Nachefski.)

T. S. S. „Zeeland"
Length 580 feet. Beam 60 feet.
Tonnage 11,904 gross.

the turn of the century.

The ability of the Polish people to maintain their culture in Europe despite the cruel rule of the Russians, Austrians, and Germans impressed St. Louis librarians. In their annual report of 1912-13, the librarians stated, "And as they have kept to themselves and to their own language in Europe, so do they insist on their social unity here in the land of their adoption." Among the Poles using the club rooms of the libraries, were the members of the Polish Women and Children Society. That organization taught English to the immigrants fresh from their homeland, and revived the Polish language among those of the second and third generation born in this country.

The librarians, as outside observers, witnessed Polish St. Louisans preserving their distinctive culture and community, while becoming Americans. Perhaps a sign of that Americanization was Polish St. Louisan Theodore S. Koziatek enlisting as a Private in the Missouri National Guard. He was only 16 years-old when he joined the Guard in January of 1913. The following April, John J. Krzyzanowski of St. Hedwig Parish joined the Missouri National Guard. Born in 1893, Krzyzanowski described himself as of "Polish Descent."

The World Falling Apart

When the Crunden Library was opened in 1909, at the corner of 14th Street and Cass Avenue on the near North Side, a company of Polish cadets drilled regularly in the auditorium. They were preparing to fight for Poland's freedom. Librarian Josephine Gratiaa described the concept of the Poles readying for the fight for freedom as, "it seemed a quixotic idea,…"

Soon, however, Poland would be one of the battlefields of World War I, as its sons would be forced to fight in opposing armies. Ironically, its nationhood and identity would hang in the balance.

On the eve of World War I erupting in Europe, 28-year-old St. Louisan Joseph Klein enlisted in the American military. Enlisting in April of 1914, Klein was one of the many self-proclaimed Polish-Americans who were building the Armed Forces of the United States.

On June 18, 1914, Archduke Francis Ferdinand was assassinated in Sarajevo — rocking the fragile peace, alliances and balance of power.

▶ Polish school children from St. Casimir Parish did their home work at the Crunden Library. This photo shows the Children's Room of the library branch overflowing with the sons and daughters of neighborhood immigrants. (Photo courtesy of Special Collections, St. Louis Public Library.)

The assassination triggered a chain of terrifying events — punitive measures against Serbia, ultimatums by the Austro-Hungarian Empire, the Empire's alliance with Germany aggravated the tensions, Russia supported the Serbs, Russia mobilized, Germany declared war against France, Germany invaded Belgium and Luxembourg, Britain supported overrun Belgium,... In the following weeks, Montenegro and Japan joined the Allies of Great Britain, France, Russia, Serbia, Italy, and Belgium. The Ottoman Empire joined the Central Powers of Germany and Austria.

Many St. Louis Poles were recent immigrants and had brothers, cousins, and sometimes parents living in Poland — a country divided and dominated by now warring nations. Its territory split between Russia, Austria and Germany, Poland was battleground in the eastern front. Each of these nations conscripted young Poles to bolster their armies, forcing the sons of Poland to war against their brothers.

Early in the war, Polish patriots debated what scenario gave the greatest potential for liberating Poland. Some believed Russian victory most likely to lead to a free Poland. And the Russian government made promises. Other patriots supported Austria, feeling their victory most likely to allow independence for Poland. No political or military organization formed in Poland to support the Germans, since they were deemed the least likely to grant Poland its nationhood. Soon most Polish patriots would decide to ally themselves with France, Russia, and England.

The conflict in Europe created a tense political environment in St. Louis neighborhoods.

Large numbers of German-Americans lived near the Polish communities in North City and in the Mount Pleasant neighborhood of South St. Louis. Naturally they sympathized with their homeland. Germany, however, had been attempting to erase the Polish culture from the third of Poland under its rule. Many of St. Louis' Irish-Americans still hoped their homeland would gain freedom from England. They believed that if the German and Austro-Hungary alliance won, a weakened, defeated England would have to grant Ireland its freedom. The Italians supported the allies, since Italy was allied with England and France. Though President Woodrow Wilson was committed to English victory, the official message was that America would be neutral.

As trench warfare began mowing down the young men of Europe, the Polish community in St. Louis was growing in size and the number and strength of its institutions.

Polish St. Louisans were building frame and brick homes on large lots around their new parsish, St. Adalbert, in the Walnut Park neighborhood.

That year the parishioners of St. Hedwig Church built a handsome, 4-square style home to serve as the rectory. The rectory, which cost $6,000 to build, faced Pulaski at the corner of Compton Avenue

In 1915, parishioners at St. Hedwig's took up their first collection for the Polish Legions — $80.00.

Frank Gawlak and his 13 year-old son Julius emigrated from Poland in 1917. Meanwhile, Antonette Gawlak waited in Poland, while her husband and son worked and saved to raise the boat fare to bring her to this country.

The Gawlak family were some of the few eastern Europeans coming to America after the War had broken out in Europe. In 1917, the annual report for the Crunden Branch Library even stated, "One noticeable result of the war at this Branch has been the absence of newly arrived immigrants."

The location of the Crunden Branch was convenient to the Polish families living around Sts. Cyril and Methodius Church,

St. Stanislaus Parish, and St. Casimir Parish. Librarian Miss Sarah Bailey described the community that the library served, which overlapped the Polish settlements. She stated that the library was in a, "section of the city where factories touch elbows with tenements, in which Poles, Italians, Russians and Jews find their homes. There are Germans in this district also, but they would be disgusted if classed with foreigners. There are also a few Lithuanians,…"

Police Sergeant Julius Trojanowski, then in his mid-60's, was still keeping the streets of St. Louis safe.

Trojanowski was patrolling the southeast end of the City, in the Carondelet neighborhood, on the night of November 2, 1917. About 3:00 a.m., a Mrs. Lang, who lived near the Mississippi River, awakened. She looked out the rear window to see a light in her poultry house and immediately woke her husband. When he saw the light, he fired a shot in the direction of the shed. Then a man escaped out the rear gate, with two suitcases in hand.

▶ An advertising card for a euchre and dance held at the Polish American Hall. (Courtesy of Carondelet Historical Society.)

Trojanowski ran toward the sound of the gunshots and saw the man fleeing with the suitcases. He fired two shots at the fleeing man, who dropped his loot to elude the officer.

Trojanowski freed the 18 chickens stashed in the suitcases. Mrs. Lang identified the chicks as coming from her hen house. It was assumed that the thief was the notorious Carondelet chicken thief, who had recently stolen several hundred chickens from Carondelet hen houses.

The news from Europe invaded the thoughts of local Poles. It was the news of nations becoming entrenched in a war of attrition, and of great armies shedding blood and grinding to a halt. St. Hedwig parishioners proudly noted that one of their young men, Anthony Szuba, was serving in the Polish Army fighting with the Allies.

At the same time, members of the United States Army, including some Polish-St. Louisans, were facing a very different challenge. Mexico's rebel leader Pancho Villa was making raids into the United States. He led an attack on Columbus, New Mexico, and executed 16 mining engineers, all U.S. Nationals. President Woodrow Wilson responded by ordering General John Pershing to invade northern Mexico to track down Pancho Villa.

As a result, young Theodore S. Koziatek of North St. Louis was serving on the Mexican Border and John J. Krzyzanowski, who had joined the Missouri National Guard, became a member of Pershing's "Mexican Expeditionary Forces."

The Yanks Are Coming

When America entered the World War in the spring of 1917, so many members of the Polish Falcons joined the American Armed Services that the local chapter almost dissolved.

U. S. General John Pershing had been recalled from Mexico, where he had been leading 4,800 American troops attempting to capture rebel leader Pancho Villa. His new mission would be to lead the American Expeditionary force in Europe.

Europe was exhausted from three years of hostilities. The new machinery of war — artillery, poisonous gases, and machine guns — were mowing down soldiers, erasing a whole generation of young Frenchmen, Germans, Englishmen, Austrians, … The Russian empire was disintegrating into its own violent revolution. The cities of the German and the Austrian empire were filled with the malnourished and starving. Huge sectors in France, Poland and Belgium were wasted by battles and bombs that had turned forests and fields into a landscape of endless, pocked, mud.

While the empires of Europe kept waging yet another offensive, desperate to win the war and end the carnage, the United States began to build, train, and equip an army.

The "Yanks" who were preparing to head, "Over There," were a whole new breed of Americans. Their ranks included descendants of families who had fought in the American Revolution as well as European immigrants and first generation Irishmen, Germans, Italians, Bohemians, … and Poles.

Many Polish St. Louisans were enlisting without need of a draft. Their families, who walked between the English and Polish languages, would soon be scanning the local papers for exotic-sounding French locations, to learn the fate of their loved ones.

On June 7, 1917, an alumnus of St. Stanislaus Grade School, John F. Kowalski, enlisted in Troop B. of the 13th Cavalry.

Kowalski would not be sent to the battlefields of Europe. Instead, the 21 year-old Missouri-born son of Polish immigrants was sent to the Mexican Border. The German government had made overtures to the Mexican government to make war together, and to make peace together. The Germans encouraged the Mexican officials with the understanding that Mexico could reconquer part of the southwestern United States. Polish-St. Louisan John Kowalski would be stationed with the troops on the Mexican border for a year and a half.

A few days after Kowalski enlisted, U.S. General John Pershing landed in Europe with the first contingents of the American Expeditionary Force.

Though inexperienced, and needing English equipment, the American troops would radically change the equation of the war in Europe, and change the morale. "..the very presence of these tall, cheerful, well-fed boys from the Middle West with their boundless optimism convinced their weary allies that the war could not now be lost. More important, it convinced their yet more weary adversaries it could not now be won," English historian Michael Howard stated.

More St. Louis Poles were donning the uniform of the American Doughboy.

▲ Polish immigrants found books on becoming United States citizens at the Crunden Library. This photo of the "Legal Advisory Board" in a meeting room of the Crunden Library is dated December 28, 1917 (Photo courtesy of Special Collections, St. Louis Public Library.)

Polish-born Bronislaus Jastrzemski became a corporal in the 56th Infantry, Company G, 7th Division. Born in 1882, he emigrated with his family in 1892. Jastrzemski had attended St. Stanislaus Parish Grade School. By the time he entered the service, he had become an asbestos worker. He was a member of the Knights of Columbus and of the Holy Name Society of St. Hedwig Parish.

Bernard Joseph Kuchiski, of 1723 N. 13th Street, joined the United States Navy and headed for the North Sea. As a Navy Seaman, Frank Wisneski, of 1920 Dodier Street, was heading to Vladivostok, Siberia and the Philippine Islands.

In December, mechanic Frank Patrick Kratchen joined the United States Navy. The Missouri-born son of immigrants from German-ruled Poland, Kratchen, had attended St. Patrick School.

By the beginning of 1918, there were already a million American troops in France. Though they were not yet organized in fighting formations, the Expeditionary Force would operate as a distinct army. They were to secure the far right of the Allied line in Lorraine.

Shoe worker Jacob Karwowski, who lived on North 10th Street, joined Company 40, Field Hospital in March of 1918. St. Stanislaus School alumnus, John J. Kwiatkowski, enlisted in July. The 31 year-old Polish-American had labored as a flour packer.

Twenty-four year-old teamster, Sylvester Kowalski, a neighbor of Karwowski, enlisted in the U.S. Infantry on April 1, 1918. He had attended St. Stanislaus School and listed his nationality as Polish.

While these Polish-St. Louisians were training, the Army of Austria-Hungary, hungry and ragged, had been gradually disintegrating into its separate ethnic elements. This fragile army was pushed into an offensive into Italy on June 15, resulting in the loss of 143,000 men. Though the remaining soldiers were sick and starving, the Central Powers were not ready to

▶ Young Ann, Charles and Mary (left to right) Krasnicki. With so many young men from the neighborhood serving in the American Armed Forces, two of the children were dressed in then fashionable sailor suits. (Photo courtesy of Roger Krasnicki.)

surrender.

St. Hedwig Parish took part in "National War Savings Day," to help finance the American war effort. The mailmen notified everyone in the neighborhood that the parish was hosting a meeting on June 28, 1918. At the meeting, a speaker encouraged these Polish-Americans and their neighbors to buy War Savings Stamps, known as Thrift Stamps, to help equip the American Army.

A month later, the Allies began a general advance on all fronts. General Pershing's force now numbered 42 U.S. divisions fighting on the right of the Allied line. By attacking northwards through the Argonne Forest, Pershing threatened the main railway line that fed the German armies.

For four years there had been bloody battles, each accompanied with prophesies of an imminent German defeat. So as the British attacked from the left, the French kept up pressure on the center of the line, and the Americans attacked on the right, few believed the Central Powers were near collapse. Instead, the Allied generals were planning their campaign for the following year — 1919. And America continued to mobilize.

Frank and Frances Kania, who had emigrated from Russian-ruled Poland, saw their son John join the U.S. Navy in August of 1918. John, whose parents had housed a boarder to help pay the bills, had attended St. Louis University. At their home in North City, the Kania family waited for news of the war and from their son.

In August, Jacob Karwowski was already engaged in the battles in Alsace.

The new offensive forced the Germans into a fighting retreat — all the way to the Hindenburg line. But the costs to the allies were again staggering — the British a further 190,000 losses and 100,000 French losses.

Another offensive, all along the line, was ordered on September 3.

The next day, Joseph Kenski, the son of Polish immigrants William and Emelia, enlisted. He was sent to "Replacement Training Camp" in Texas. A clerk who lived on North 18th Street, Kenski had attended public grade schools and then continued his education at night school.

In mid-September, the American Expeditionary Corps' First Army, and the French Corps, launched an attack at St. Mihiel to the south of Verdun. It had been held continuously by the Germans since 1914.

Among the American forces fighting at St. Mihiel were graduates of St. Stanislaus grade school, Sylvester Kowalski, and Theodore S. Koziatek, who had served with Pershing on the Mexican border.

The German resistance was collapsing. By September 16, American troops had captured 15,000 German prisoners. The Americans had suffered 7,000 casualties. On September 26, General Pershing launched the Meuse-Argonne offensive, north of Verdun. Pershing's First Army, numbering one million men, was holding 17 miles of the front line. They made rapid gains, while the Germans rushed reinforcements to the sector.

The following day British and French forces assaulted the main Hindenburg line, firing a barrage of nearly a million shells in 24 hours. Since the beginning of August, the German army had lost a further 228,000 men, half of them through desertion. Though defeat threatened the Central Powers, the war and the casualties continued.

Martha Gayeski lived in the second floor unit at 4418a Evans Avenue in North City when her husband, Theodore, was killed in the Battle of the Argonne, on October 1, 1918. A mechanic by trade, 23 year-old Gayeski had been serving in Company B., 138th Infantry, 35th Division.

Fighting through the Meuse, Argonne Forests were Theodore Koziatek, who had been promoted to the rank of 2nd Lieutenant, and then 2nd Lieutenant John J. Krzyzanowski, whose home was at 4702 Compton in the Mount Pleasant neighborhood.

Polish St. Louisan, shoeworker Jacob Karwowski, fought in the next stage of the offensive beginning on October 14. St. Louis Pole Florian O. Brinbinski was killed in action on the day after the offensive was launched.

November 1, American troops led the third and final stage of the Meuse-Argonne Offensive. That day, only ten days before truce ended the conflict, Corporal Bronislaus Jastrzemski, also known as Barney Jastrzemski of Company G., 56th Infantry, 7th Division, was killed in action in France. The Polish immigrant was the son of John and Katherine Jastrzemski of St. Hedwig Parish.

St. Stanislaus graduate, 31 year-old John Kwiatkowski, was wounded at the Argonne Forest on November 6. The Polish, St. Louis teamster Sylvester Kowalski was again at the battlelines, in the Meuse Argonne offensive, through to November 11, 1918.

During the fighting at Verdun, all of the officers of St. Louisan Leo Kowalkowski's Battalion had been killed or wounded. Kowalkowski was in the center of fire twice when he went after his wounded captain, and was chased by German patrols. Undaunted, he tried again. With bullets flying and shells bursting around him, he carried the captain through "No Man's Land" to safety. The St. Louis Star reported that Kowalkowski braved enemy fire three times to rescue his captain.

Armistice was declared on November 11, 1918.

There is no tally of the number of Polish St. Louisans who served in World War I. Records remaining with former St. Hedwig parishioners counted 62 young men from their parish who enlisted in the American Army. A memorial plaque was installed at the Crunden Library honoring the citizens of the City's Fourth Ward who had died in the war. The list included Frolian Obremski, Stanislaus Rykowski, John Mikolajeski and Peter Nowak.

The numbers killed in the war was beyond comprehension — 115,000 American troops,

740,000 English, 170,000 from the British empire, 1,400,000 French, 1,700,000 Russians, 1,800,000 Germans, 1,200,000 from Austria-Hungary. The numbers of Poles killed were not counted separately, but counted with the empires which had ruled them.

In the path between German and Russian armies, much of Poland had been decimated. By January 1, 1919, St. Hedwig parishioners had collected $6,000. for the cause of Poland. Poles in St. Louis and in the homeland could take some comfort in that after 124 years of oppression by Kaisers, Emperors and Czars, Poland was again an independent nation.

On July 8, 1919, Leo Kowalkowski was notified that he had been awarded the distinguished service cross for bravery at Verdun. Kowalkowski, who was living at 1321 North 20th Street, only a block south of St. Stanislaus Parish, did not seem enthusiastic about the recognition. He was more concerned that he had not been able to find a job.

Since the demobilization of his unit earlier that year, Kowalkowski had been tramping the streets of St. Louis looking for work. "What I want is a job. I almost got one the other day, but when I went to accept it I found that a married woman had beat me to it. I was out of luck."

He reluctantly told a reporter from the St. Louis Star how he had rescued a wounded captain under fire. "But say, that's nothing," he told the reporter. "Just tell somebody to give me a chance to make good." He stated, "There are a lot of things I can do, for I was only gassed."

▼ The dedication ceremonies for the plaque at the Crunden Library honoring neighborhood residents killed in the World War. The ceremony was held on Armistice Day, November 11, 1921. (Photo courtesy of Special Collections, St. Louis Public Library.)

The Prosperous Twenties

After the "War to End All Wars," the Sutkowski family permanently settled in North St. Louis City. They had moved to East St. Louis several times, so the father and grandfather could walk to their jobs at the foundries. But their young daughter Milainia had trouble breathing due to the severe pollution caused by the mills on the East Side. After the family returned to St. Louis, their fourth child, Chester was born.

Though American-born, the first language of the four Sutkowski children was Polish. They ate Polish food, sang Polish hymns, and grew up in Sts. Cyril and Methodius Church.

The federal census of 1920 counted 5,224 St. Louisans whose birthplace was Poland. But the community that spoke the language, enjoyed the traditions and practiced the religions — like the Sutkowski children — was much larger.

Estimates of the real size of the Polish community on the eve of the prosperous 1920's appeared in the annual report of the St. Louis Public Library. In 1919, librarian Josephine Gratiaa stated, "Estimates of the number now in the city vary from twelve to thirty thousand. The Poles originally settled in the district in which the Crunden Branch of the Library is located." The librarian described the Polish Roman Catholic Churches near the Crunden Library as flourishing. She also noted the growth in the Polish National Catholic Church, which claimed a membership of over a hundred families.

▼ A formal portrait of the Krasnicki family. (Photo courtesy of Roger Krasnicki.)

To serve that north side Polish community, "There is a collection of about 630 Polish books in the Crunden Branch." In addition to carrying St. Louis' Polish language weekly, the Przewodnik Polski or Polish Guide, the library subscribed to Polish dailies from Milwaukee and Chicago. The library also received the English language publication Free Poland, but it was not as popular as the Polish language publications.

"It is true of the Poles as of most foreigners that the children use the library more than the adults. The Polish man comes frequently to get books on citizenship, otherwise, unless American born, he reads Polish books exclusively. The Polish woman comes for crochet books and books in her mother tongue."

"The children use the library for a place in which to prepare their lessons; every evening sees at least one table of Polish boys and girls working away at their arithmetic," Gratiaa stated. Since each of the Polish churches had a hall and, "...the Polish-American Hall at 19th and Cass Ave. shelters practically all the Polish societies and lodges in St. Louis," Gratiaa added that the Poles seldom used the meeting rooms at the library.

She described the employment found by the Polish men as, "'heavy work,'...meaning shop work of all kinds; foundry and rolling-mill work. There are however ... small shopkeepers, and in the Crunden neighborhood there are many saloons kept by Poles."

She credited the Poles of North City with being "law-abiding and peaceful people, but clannish." The librarians found it difficult to get the Poles to talk, because they were shy about trying to express themselves in English.

◄ The first communion photo of Genevieve Lubaszewski Zygmunt of St. Casimir Parish. The J.J. Belka Studio of North St. Louis City took the photos of many of the special events in St. Casimir Parish. (Photo courtesy of Bernice Krauze.)

That reticence made it, "a unique experience when a young Polish woman told us with pride that her husband did beautiful embroidery," Gratiaa stated. "When astonishment and incredulity were expressed, she brought samples of his work to the library and explained that in the 'old country' where he had learned, many of the men embroidered the gayly-colored borders of their smocks."

The children in this Polish community were growing up in a world in which, although their native language was Polish, English was spoken at both Catholic and public schools, shopkeepers spoke Yiddish, or German, or Italian, or Polish, and nearby parishes served Irish immigrants or their descendants.

▼ Rows of Polish school children in early 1920's. (Photo courtesy of Bernice Krauze.)

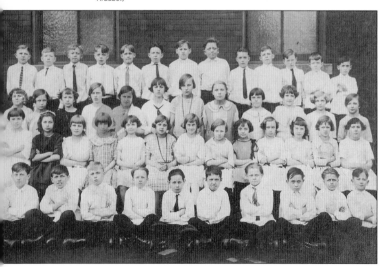

Mrs. Sutkowski shopped at the Ellerbrock's German Bakery. She frequented a dry goods store and shoe store on Biddle Street, where many Jewish merchants had shops. At most of these stores the shopkeeper or one of the clerks spoke Polish and could accommodate the Polish customers.

Though many in the community spoke Polish, easing the transition for new immigrants, there were still many challenges for the recent immigrants. Some of the immigrants who lived near the Sutkowski's home found jobs in the huge tobacco factories near 39th Street and Park Avenue, on the south side of the City. Though the factories were conveniently served by streetcars, many of the immigrants walked two to four miles each way to and from the factories. The walk, however, was not to save money. The immigrants, unable to read the English names of the streetcar lines, were afraid of taking the wrong car and getting lost.

Starting kindergarten at Douglas School at 11th and Howard Streets was a shock for Milainia Sutkowski. "It sounded so funny when the teacher asked me my name in English." It was at Douglas School that Milainia learned the English language.

In addition to caring for her family, Mrs. Sutkowski kept a stall at Biddle Market, where she sold chickens and turkeys. While at the market with her daughter, Milainia would, "stop at the place that sold sauerkraut. The man made the kraut at the market. He had a piano. He would let me play it. I was fascinated."

The stability, wealth and comfort of the North Side Polish community was strengthened in 1922 by the founding of Pulaski Building and Loan Association. Local Poles had pooled their resources to form the association which provided loans, mortgages, and conducted real estate transactions. During its early years, Polish American grocers, a florist and a member of the St. Louis Police Department were active with the building and loan. Julian Pilinski, president of the association, lived less than one city block south of St. Stanislaus Church. The association's offices were also in the neighborhood, on Cass Avenue only four blocks from the Polish Hall.

Meanwhile, St. Casimir Parish School had been averaging 650 children since 1910. That vibrant parish community on the near North Side included approximately 600 families.

The nuns from St. Casimir grade school insisted that every child in the school have a library card. Librarian for the Crunden Branch, Miss Sarah Bailey, recognized the efforts of the nuns. She stated, "The amount of trouble these nuns take in this connection is remarkable. They not only select the books, but keep all the children's cards with a list of the books charged on them and see that they are renewed or returned on the date due."

During the three years immediately following the war, St. Hedwig's parishioners gave $2,127. for the people of Poland left destitute by their nation being used as a battlefield. In addition, the ladies of the parish collected about $4,000 worth of clothing and necessities to send to Poland.

In the spring of 1922, more than three years after Barney Jastrzemski was killed in France, his body was brought home to his

▼ The first Board of Directors of Pulaski Building and Loan (later Pulaski Bank) in 1922. Seated (left to right) are John Trzecki, Frank Obremski, Stanley Ciborowski, Julian Pilinski, Anton Lassa, and Thomas Przybylski. Standing are Frank Nawrocki, Stanley Wardenski, A. Hausch, Joseph Laskowski, Michael MierzFwinski, A. Brys, and Anton Turek.

family. The body was taken to the parlor of the Central Undertaking Company on Cass Avenue, where it laid in state, then was moved to the family residence at 3224 Itaska Street, across the street from St. Hedwig Church. The funeral mass was held at the Polish church, and the body interred with full military honors at SS. Peter and Paul's Cemetery.

The following year, the visit to St. Louis by General Josef Haller, hero of the Great War and Commander of the new Polish Army, became more than an official visit to encourage trade and good will between the new republic of Poland and the United States. It became a celebration of the Polish community in St. Louis.

About 7:30 a.m., on Wednesday, October 31, 1923, General Josef Haller, arrived in St. Louis by train. The American Legion hosted the visit, which included visits with the Mayor, the Archbishop, a motor tour of St. Louis, an address to the Chamber of Commerce, and speeches delivered in English, French and Polish. That evening the American Legion, the Polish Veterans' Association, the Military Order of the World War, and the Reserve Officers' Association held a banquet at the Hotel Statler on Washington Avenue to honor the general. Among those praising the general was former Judge Frank Groski, president of the Polish Citizen Association.

The dinner not only recognized the General's role in the First World War, but also for organizing the Army of the new Polish Republic, and overwhelmingly defeating the Bolshevik offensive against Poland in August of 1920. Haller, in turn, honored the 120,000 Boy Scouts of Poland who voluntarily entered the national army to take up arms against the Bolshevik offensive.

Thursday morning Haller attended mass at St. Hedwig Parish on Pulaski Street, where Barney Jastrzemski's funeral mass had been held. Newspaper articles indicate that Haller had planned to attend mass at the Cathedral on Lindell, but opted to go to little St. Hedwig Polish Parish. After mass, his motorcade headed south on Broadway to inspect the troops and quarters at Jefferson Barracks.

That evening, Haller had dinner with the Polish-American war veterans, at the Polish Hall at 1940 Cass Avenue. The *Globe-Democrat* estimated the crowd welcoming him to the hall at 3,000. There he gave, an "address in his native tongue to a large gathering of compatriots," according to the *Post-Dispatch*. Afterwards, there was a reception at the home of Dr. and Mrs. Marion Wachowiak at their home at 5933 Waterman Avenue in the West End.

The morning of Friday, November 2, Haller left St. Louis for Springfield, Illinois, to lay a wreath at the tomb of Abraham Lincoln.

In the Walnut Park neighborhood of North St. Louis, Poles had built an arts and crafts style, two-story rectory for St. Adalbert Parish. In 1923, they also constructed an addition to their humble St. Adalbert church — a steel framed belfry. The following year, the small Polish community around St. Adalbert Church managed to build and open their own parish school. On July 16, 1924, the city issued the parish a permit to build the brick school, with an estimated cost of $30,000. On July 27th, the cornerstone was laid for the new school.

More bungalows were being constructed around St. Adalbert Church. Names appearing on the building permits included Fublanski, Benthowski, and Palczynski. "F. Groszoski," sometimes spelled Groszewski,

appeared as the contractor for church buildings and homes in the immediate area.

While the Poles in Walnut Park were building schools and houses, the Polish children in the Frenchtown neighborhood were required to attend Mass every morning before classes began at Our Lady of Czestochowa School. The children recited prayers before and after each class as well as recess and starting and ending classes. Classes were taught in both English and Polish. "The children were obliged to read and write in English and Polish, besides learn the Catechism, Church History, World History, Geography, Arithmetic, in both languages;…" according to Hania Turek.

The women parishioners cleaned the church and school, bringing their own lye soap and buckets, as well as large scrub brushes to clean the wooden floors and desks. The children took turns cleaning the blackboards and emptying the trash.

"The people were hard-working but they enjoyed themselves with house parties; they loved Polish music and dancing. Someone always knew how to play a violin or an accordion. The women were good cooks,…" Turek recorded.

◄ School girls pose with one of the sisters in the brick-edged garden of St. Casimir Parish. (Photo courtesy of Roger Krasnicki.)

▲ Members of the Polish National Choirs overflowed the stage of the Polish Hall. American symbols, the Stars and Stripes and portrait of George Washington, were prominently displayed in this center of Polish-American culture. (Photos courtesy of Sts. Cyril and Methodius Church.)

In old North St. Louis, Mrs. Sutkowski had given up her stall at the Biddle Street Market to work at a laundry. But young Milainia had not lost her fascination with the piano she used to play at the market. Her father bought her a piano, that was in bad shape, from a railroad salvage yard and put it in the shed. Every morning before she walked to school, Milania went out to the shed, and with one finger, she played the Star Spangled Banner.

Milainia started taking piano lessons with a local piano teacher, Lillian Doyle. Young Milainia knew Doyle was Irish, "because she let you know she was Irish." Doyle was assistant organist at the nearby Irish Catholic Church, St. Michael. During piano lessons, Doyle would ask Milainia catechism questions. Milainia had learned her catechism in Polish. "So while I was taking piano lessons, I had to translate catechism answers from Polish to English."

The neighborhood saloons around the Sutkowski's home in Old North St. Louis sold "near beer" from Anheuser Busch, but some also offered their own home brew. "Somebody always warned them when the Feds were coming. Then they would get rid of the home brew and just put out the near beer," according to Elsie Sutkowski Bratkowski.

The Polish people of St. Louis expressed and demonstrated great loyalty to their homeland, and to their chosen country, the United States. There was one law that they, like their Irish, German, Italian, Bohemian,… American neighbors, believed absurd. Many of these otherwise law-abiding St. Louisans simply ignored Prohibition. Passed in 1919, it prohibited the production or sale of liquor, wine or beer.

Polish American Max Misko operated an ice cream parlor in the handsome storefront at 1748 Chouteau, at 18th Street. He and his wife Catharine lived in the apartment over the "parlor." Relatives and friends, however, described his business as a speakeasy.

A young Polish boy, whose family lived on Palm Street, didn't think too much about his dad and his friends setting up equipment in the kitchen. There were coils that dripped, dripped, dripped, a clear liquid into five gallon crocks. But then his father and his friends worked at Malinkrodt Chemical, which seemed to the young son to explain the technical activity going on in the kitchen.

There were, however, some interesting behaviors surrounding the dripping gizmo in the kitchen. Occasionally, someone would knock at the door, and then the men would quickly dismantle the coils and equipment. When the police came around shortly after that, smelling some sort of fumes, nothing was in the kitchen.

▲ Members of the Polish folk dance troupe of St. Hedwig Parish.

A Polish mother wrapped bottles, filled with an unknown liquid, in newspaper. She then put them in a shoe box and directed her daughter to deliver the shoe box to a household near the Shrine of St. Joseph. The daughter never asked what she was delivering.

In the Polish settlement around 7th and 8th Streets and Cass Avenue, a Polish family pushed a baby carriage around the neighborhood, and by St. Patrick and St. Casimir Churches. Tucked under the baby blankets were bottles of liquor prepared for delivery to families on the route.

When federal agents surprised another Polish household in the neighborhood, the lady of the house quickly grabbed the baby and then sat down on the vat containing the bootleg. She discretely spread her long skirt, hiding the vat. As agents searched her home, she rocked and soothed the baby, whispering "sshh, sshh."

Joseph Penski, a laborer who lived at 1438 North 10th Street, was one of the Poles who made his own brew during Prohibition. Evidently he occasionally made an extra jug for a friend, because at least once he sent his son Stanley to deliver his gift. Stanley, barely a teenager, carried the jug onto the streetcar. While sitting on the rolling and rocking car, the illegal brew started to audibly slosh around in the jug. Young Stanley was horrified, wondering if the other streetcar riders would realize that he was delivering illegal booze.

Though jobs were plentiful, it was still difficult to raise a family on a workingman's wage. To help keep their home warm, Mary Penski used to walk along the railroad tracks gathering the lumps of coal that had fallen from railroad cars. She walked to produce row where she collected the bruised or overripe produce that had been cast aside. These she used to make soup.

The many small city parks and playgrounds were focal points in the Polish children's play and social life. It seemed that almost all the Polish children of St. Stanislaus Parish played baseball in Murphy's Playground, a small park on the corner of 20th

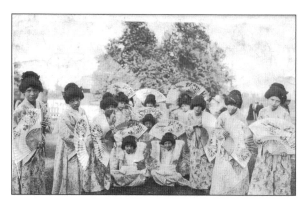

▲ The Polish-American children of St. Casimir Parish costumed in Japanese garb for the school play. (Photo courtesy of Roger Krasnicki.)

Street and Cass Avenue. Many of the children of Sts. Cyril and Methodius Polish National Catholic Church played in Strodtman Park, and enjoyed the summer crafts programs offered there.

On summer evenings, neighbors socialized on the front steps. After supper and after the dishes were washed, "everyone spilled out on the steps. The kids would play jump rope, hop-scotch. The older folks would talk about their daily problems," according to Elsie Sutkowski Bratkowski.

Though Milania's piano playing provided musical entertainment for the family, her uncle brought over a crystal set radio. The family used to pass around the earphones and listen. Little Elsie thought the radio was a miracle.

◄ Members of Sts. Cyril and Methodius Polish National Catholic Church posed on the steps of their historic church building, at 9th and Chambers Streets in North St. Louis, in 1929. (Photo courtesy of Sts. Cyril and Methodius Church.)

practiced dentistry at his office on Cass Avenue and Frank B. Grodzki who took care of the legal needs of Polish families at his Cass Avenue office.

Mr. Sutkowski had been buying property. Eventually he owned three of the four corners at Blair Avenue and Monroe Avenue. Gradually he had been doing more and more maintenance work on his buildings, and learning the construction trades. Finally, he was able to leave the mills, and work full-time on building maintenance and construction.

The new prosperity of working-class Polish families was reflected by their buying automobiles — a luxury when they lived in convenient neighborhoods served well by streetcars. Mr. F. Kosakowski even hired A. Seitoski, a builder, to construct a garage at his home at 3334 Blair, in North City. Another sign of financial security was that Polish families were now posing for photos for special occasions at Boleslaw Buben's studio on Mullanphy Street. The community was served by its own professionals, including Dr. Walter Grodzki who

Interest in the St. Louis Falcons had been rekindled in 1925, and in 1928, the nest sent a large contingent of athletes to participate in the National Meet in Syracuse, New York.

On February 3, 1928, fire ravaged the sanctuary of St. Stanislaus Church. Fortunately, the 18th century replica of the icon of Our Lady of Czestochowa and its marble altar had survived the disaster. The fire, however, had cracked and shattered the art glass windows and almost completely destroyed the sanctuary. Insurance covered only part of the $60,000 in damages.

The people of St. Stanislaus Parish restored their church with distinctive artistry and craftmanship. Polish St. Louisan Michael Olszewski, whose stained glass studio was in his Virginia Avenue storefront, created the

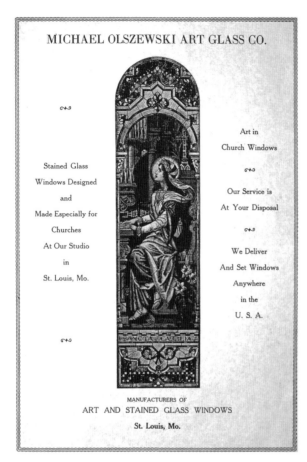

▲ An advertisement for the Michael Olszewski Art Glass Company of St. Louis. The company crafted the stained glass windows of St. Stanislaus Church. The Olszewski family were among the early members of St. Stanislaus Parish.

brilliantly colored new windows for the church. New stenciling ornamented the walls. And a copy of what at that time was the world's largest painting of the crucifixion was installed in the blind arcade of the apse. A Polish artist, Jan Styka, had painted the original panorama of the cruxifixion for the St. Louis World's Fair.

While the people of St. Stanislaus were restoring their church, life in the Polish community of the Mount Pleasant neighborhood continued to revolve around parish organizations and neighborhood businesses.

The hardwork and successes of the Poles in St. Louis did not protect them from the distrust, disdain and even hatred of some American nativists. The Ku Klux Klan, peaking in its power and influence, was terrorizing African-Americans, Jews, Catholics and immigrants. A threat, in the language of the Klan, was left at St. Hedwig Church on Saturday, September 19, 1925.

About 10:30 at night, two men planted a four-foot tall cross in the lawn of St. Hedwig Roman Catholic Church in the Mount Pleasant neighborhood. The cross was wrapped in oil-soaked burlap. The men set the cross on fire, then fled in a touring car.

Frank Jankowski of 3227 Pulaski Street saw the flaming sybol of the Ku Klux Klan's hatred. He ran to the church yard, took the flaming cross from the yard and threw it into the paved street, where its embers could die rather than spread flames. The Carondelet News reported that he, "pursued the machine in which the men were riding to Compton

The founders of St. Hedwig Parish gathered on their church steps for the 25th anniversary of their parish. Pictured in the first row (left to right) are J. Wisniewski, A. Marchlewski, Reverend Stepka, M. Sikorska, and M. Kalinowski. Pictured in the middle row are J. Pytlinski, Wm. Doetzel, J. Kalinowski, J. Marchlewski, J. Kwiatkowski, and J. Trudzinski. Pictured in the top row are F. Marchlewski, A. Kaszewski, F. Kalinowski and Apolonia Jastrzemski Niedzielska, whose brother Bronislaus had died in the World War.

Ladies of St. Hedwig Parish demonstrated their humor and creativity by making a "cello" out of a laundry tub and a "horn" out of tincans for instruments for their kitchen band. The background indicates the open, undeveloped lots and parcels in the Mount Pleasant neighborhood of South City in 1929. (Photo courtesy of John and Theresa Blaskiewicz.)

avenue, where he lost sight of it."

As his daughters were growing up, Jankowski chose not to speak to them about the incident and what it symbolized.

Though the family moved several times, the Jankowski family always lived close to St. Hedwig Parish. The children played hopscotch, jumping rope, lay-low sheep, and tag in nearby, blocksized Mount Pleasant Park.

On Saturday night the Jankowski sisters, Helen, Florentine, and Anna Marie, washed their hair and put it up in curlers so they would look their best for Sunday Morning mass. Sunday evening, family members gathered to

play cards. On warm evenings, many Polish families carried the kitchen chairs and a card table to the front porch, where they played pinochle.

A Polish butcher with a shop on Cass Avenue, Imbierowicz, opened another shop two blocks from St. Hedwig Church, to serve that Polish community. The Kalinowski family opened Quality Hardware on Virginia Avenue. The family lived over their shop. Polish-American attorney Tom Krauska advised many of his fellow St. Hedwig parishioners at his office at 4603 Virginia. Michael Olszewski's Art Glass Company operated its studio at 4644 Virginia.

As the prosperous 1920's were coming to

a close, St. Hedwig Parish was thriving. The roster numbered 240 parish families. And their graduates were working their way into the medical professions. In 1924, Anthony A. Piekarski graduated from St. Louis University's School of Medicine. He had graduated from St. Hedwig grade school in 1913. In 1928, St. Hedwig alumnus Roman H. Stranz graduated from St. Louis University's School of Medicine and joined the staff of St. Mary's Hospital. Another St. Hedwig alumnus, Thaddeus Nowak, graduated from St. Louis University's Dental School in 1929.

The parish boasted a sewing circle, a kitchen band, a dramatic club, a girls' basketball team, dance troupes, a choir, a dozen religious organizations and clubs, a chapter of the St. Vincent dePaul Society to carry out charitable efforts, a chapter of the Polish National Alliance which sponsored several trophy winning parish teams, a dramatic club, and an orchestra.

February 6, 1929, the St. Hedwig parish orchestra, which included eight violinists, a flautist and a boy in knickers playing a saxophone, gave a concert at the Hotel Melbourne. The concert was aired for radio station "WIL, the Friendly Station."

Though many Polish-Americans continued to work long hours, at demanding physical

▲ The 1929 St. Stanislaus Parish Grade School graduates with their diplomas in hand.

work, often in dangerous factories, overall the community was enjoying new economic security. This new wealth was recognized by the White Star Steamer Line. The steamship line was marketing their oceanliner trips to Poland, via England, to the St. Louis Polish community.

At the same time that the Polish St. Louis community was growing and its organizations and cultural institutions gaining vitality, its future was being stunted. In 1924, the United States had developed new immigration policies that were checking the growth of the Polish community in St. Louis.

Hard Times Are Not To The Poles

he Stock Market Crash on Thursday, October 24, 1929, so devastated the economy that the day of the crash was named "Black Thursday." Frightened investors, selling at any price, traded nearly 13 million shares that day. After frenzied, panicked selling of stock, dazed brokers waded through paper on the floor of the New York stock exchange —trying to add up their losses. Those losses were in the billions. Thousands of accounts were wiped out. The stock market crash gradually rippled through the economy, and across the nation.

As the effects of the crash and subsequent economic depression crept into their lives and their community, Polish-St. Louisans responded with resilience. The Federal Census of 1930 documented 5,198 Polish-born residents in the City of St. Louis.

With the diminished role of immigration in St. Louis, due to federal restrictions, many more city residents were American-born. Of the just over 800,000 city residents, only 80,000 were foreign born. German-born Americans, numbering 22,000, made up the largest number of foreign-born. The nearly 10,000 Russian-born St. Louisans, the second largest number of foreign-born, included many Russian-Orthodox Christian and Jewish refugees from the Bolsevik revolution in Russia. Over 9,000 St. Louisans were natives of Italy. The Austrian and Irish immigrants numbered almost the same as the Polish, just over 5,000 each in 1930.

The African-American population of the city grew substantially during the Roaring Twenties as many left the deep South to find jobs in the expanding industries in St. Louis and other Midwestern and Northern cities. The numbers of African-Americans calling St. Louis home grew from about 70,000 to about 94,000 between 1920 and 1930.

In the face of the deepening Depression,

▲ The home of the Polish Falcons at 2013 St. Louis Avenue, originally the home of brewer Charles Stifel, before fire destroyed the upper floors. (Photo courtesy of the Polish Falcons Nest 45.)

▲ The Polish Falcons' young athletes proudly displayed their trophies on the steps of their hall on St. Louis Avenue. (Photo courtesy of the Polish Falcons Nest 45.)

President Herbert Hoover was declaring that the nation must "prevent hunger and cold" for those in real trouble.

Somehow, in the midst of such uncertain times, the Polish Falcons bought the magnificent Stifel Mansion to house their many activities in 1931. The Polish community had been spreading across more of North City during the 1920's. The three-story, Victorian era mansion was located at 2013 St. Louis Avenue, in an area built up by Irish and German immigrants during the 19th century, and becoming home to Polish families. After the death of Otto Stifel, the Evangelical Synod became the owners of the Stifel home.

The Polish Falcons paid the synod

$24,000 for the house, and its brick walled grounds that included two stables. German-American brewer Charles Stifel had built the grand home, with a stone facade, granite steps, polished granite pillars, a slate covered mansard roof, and ornate cast iron trim. The interior boasted spiral stairs, with two rooms on each side of the main hall. Miniature onyx columns enhanced the intricately- carved mantles. Originally, the third floor had been home to the household servants.

The Polish-American children, attending Falcons' activities with their parents in the old mansion, were fascinated by the dumb waiter. One little girl tried to take rides in it.

Polish St. Louisan and World War I veteran John F. Kania was promoted to the position of manager of the new business department at Cass Bank and Trust Company. The bank, at 13th Street and Cass Avenue, was wooing the Polish community with Polish language advertisements and customer service.

While most of her girlfriends had gotten work permits and jobs out of grammar school, at about age 14, Milainia Sutkowski was forturnate enough to attend high school. She graduated from Beaumont High in 1931, when more Americans were losing jobs than finding them. Millie started job hunting, but kept seeing signs that read, "No help wanted, no help wanted, no help wanted." Recalling those tough days she said, "So you had to lie. Yeah, I'm experienced. I can do that job." She found a job in an embroidery factory, working 8:00 a.m. to 5:00 p.m. for five days a week with a half hour for lunch and a half a day on Saturday. The pay was $9.00 a week. At the news of her job, her father exclaimed, "your mother came here from the old country, not knowing anything and she worked in a factory. And you, with a high school education, working in a factory?"

The Sutkowskis were enjoying the luxury of an oil furnace. But with the poor economy, and heating oil costing seven cents a gallon, their father disconnected the oil furnace. He returned to the hard work of shoveling the less expensive coal for their heat.

The piano lessons for Milainia and the cost of the piano had evolved into a wise investment for the Sutkowski family. In the fall of 1932, Milainia became the organist for Sts. Cyril and Methodius Church. The choir was growing, soon to number 50 members.

In January 1933, businessmen, investors, and then regular Americans started making large, then larger withdrawals from banks across the nation. The lack of confidence in the economy was evolving into a new, and dangerous form — a run on the banks. Each day, there were new notices of banks closing their doors. People worried should they withdraw their hard-earned savings, possibly adding to the panic, or wait and risk losing everything. By the middle of January, the panic in St. Louis was running wild.

Max Misko had become a shareholder in 12th Street National Bank at 1130 Chouteau Avenue at 12th Street. He and his wife still lived over their "ice cream parlor" just down the street at 1748 Chouteau Avenue.

On January 16, 1933, a headline in the *Post-Dispatch* read, "7 More Neighborhood Banks Close;…16 Here In Last 12 Days." The Post reported, "In each case, the decision to close was attributed to recent withdrawals by depositors, and the action taken was declared to be for the depositors' protection."

That morning a notice had appeared on the closed doors of the 12th Street National Bank, "Although it is the belief of the board of directors of the Twelfth Street National Bank of St. Louis that all depositors can be paid in full, yet in the view of the uncertain banking conditions in St. Louis, the board of directors deems it advisable for the protection of all depositors to turn over the affairs of this bank to the national bank examiner, effective this date."

Misko's savings and investments were in limbo.

Twenty-one year-old Peter Swiatek, who lived and banked on the East Side, had managed to save about $1,500. The son of Polish immigrants lost all his savings in the run on the banks.

Though banks most convenient to the Polish neighborhoods on the North Side did not close, and many Polish families had little on no savings to lose, the run on the banks froze the economy. Employers had few resources to pay employees, and many factories closed.

One out of every four heads of households — 13 million Americans — were jobless. Across the nation, farmers were being evicted. In St. Louis, families no longer able to pay the rent were building tarpaper shacks between the industries along the riverfront.

Franklin D. Roosevelt was inaugurated on March 4, 1933, stating, "the only thing we have to fear is fear itself." Through the radio, his confident voice brought some comfort and hope to suffering and anxious Americans across the country.

Many Polish St. Louisans still had no access to radios to even hear the president. It was common for Polish families to struggle through the economic castrophe by pooling and stretching their limited family resources. Entertainment was almost always free.

Milainia Sutkowski had been frugal, saving her money to marry Peter Swiatek, who had lost his savings in the run on the banks. She had saved $1,850. Her father, however, was having difficulty making the payments on one of his properties at Blair and Monroe Avenues. When the property was about to be foreclosed on, Milainia used her savings to make the payments.

In the midst of these hard times, the 1880's St. Stanislaus school building required updating to meet new codes. The renovation, which included an addition with new staircases, cost $55,000. The words "St. Stanislaus School" were cut into the stone over the new entrance with stylish, Art Deco lettering.

▲ Many Polish immigrant children learned American history and culture at the Crunden Library. During the Great Depression, WPA muralist Valentine Vogel painted this American cowboy on the wall. (Photo courtesy of Special Collections, St. Louis Public Library.)

◀ Children lined up to enter the Crunden Branch Library at Cass Avenue and 14th Street. (Photo courtesy of Special Collections, St. Louis Public Library.)

In the Frenchtown or Kosciusko neighborhood, the Rudawski family called a two family flat at 3rd and Victor Streets home. The parents and their three children had four rooms, with an outhouse.

Young Joe Rudawski played in Our Lady of Czestohowa's school yard. The school yard plus the empty lot next to it, that the neighborhood children used as a playground,

added up to a quarter city block. On Saturdays the boys walked the eight city blocks to Lyon Park. The children fished there, since the City Parks and Recreation Department stocked the pond. On weekends, the neighborhood families picnicked in the park.

In that southern end of Frenchtown, also called Kosciusko, the Polish kids all spoke English, because they were playing with other neighborhood boys whose families had come to St. Louis from Arkansas, Tennessee, and Flat River Missouri. The children played Indian ball. This variation on baseball had smaller teams — only first and second base, two infielders and two outfielders. They also played corkball and bottle caps.

On some Saturday nights the Rudawski family, children and parents, went to the show for 10 cents. Though Mr. Rudawski didn't care for the movies, Mrs. Rudawski did. The family went to the Peerless Show on South Broadway.

The other major entertainment for the boys on Saturday night was to sit around the neighborhood and tell stories. Sitting on the curb, the boys regaled each other with lots of ghost stories.

About 1936, the Rudawski family moved to a four-family flat at 410 Victor Street. The five member family shared a three room flat.

Though they had lost a room, the move was perceived as a step up, since now the Rudawski family had an indoor toilet.

Though the neighborhood around Our Lady of Czestochowa had a number of residents from other parts of the United States and Europe in addition to Poles, there were plenty of Polish shops. There was a Polish butcher shop on 4th and Sidney Streets. Tony Sadowski operated a Polish grocery at 3rd and Victor. And a Polish Tavern, Traczy's Tavern, at Broadway and Victor Streets, sold buckets of beer for 15 cents. "Sometimes, I went with my dad to Traczy's," Joe Rudawski stated. "Sometimes I'd take the bucket and get it filled and bring it home to my Dad."

▼ Scene at Murphy Park, which was located at the corner of Cass Avenue and North 20th Street. The park was a focal point of life in its Polish neighborhood. (Photo courtesy of Eleanor Podolski.)

◄ Houses, stores and flats framed Murphy Park, where neighborhood residents gathered for ball games. (Photo courtesy of Eleanor Podolski.)

▼ Tracy's Tavern at 2500 South Broadway was a favorite gathering place for the Polish men of the Frenchtown or Kosciuko neighborhood.

PRospect 9535

TRACY'S TAVERN

2500 SO. BROADWAY

On June 17, after losing his savings in the run on the banks and sharing her savings with her father, Peter Swiatek and Milainia Sutkowski were married.

The Deptula family lived in the six room flat, in the apartment building at 1402 North 20th Street, directly across the street from St. Stanislaus Church. Even during the depths of the Depression, Mr. Deptula's job at Banner Iron Company enabled the family to send their daughter Eleanor to St. Stanislaus Grade School.

In summer time, Eleanor walked to Murphy's Park, where city employees organized summer programs for the children. They had games, and arts and crafts. A big outing was a walk to Mullanphy Park, at 11th and Mullanphy Street, where the kids swam in the city indoor pool.

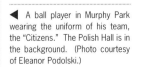

◀ A ball player in Murphy Park wearing the uniform of his team, the "Citizens." The Polish Hall is in the background. (Photo courtesy of Eleanor Podolski.)

At Christmas, a special treat was decorating the big trees set up in the church, around the manger scene. The children separated each strand of tinsel, and draped each individually across a branch.

Each Christmas eve, the church bells would start ringing at 11:30 p.m. Parishioners would walk through the cold night, along the neighborhood streets lined with their brick flats, and storefronts, and rowhouses. When they entered the church, the lights were dimmed. The crib, however, would be lit, and the tinsel on the Christmas trees around the crib reflected the light. The parishioners sang Polish hymns and carols until mass began. To the Polish-American children, with their families weathering the hardships of the Depression, these sights were magical.

Christmas morning, Eleanor Deptula would find her Christmas stocking stuffed with winter delicacies — apples, oranges, tangerines, walnuts and pecans.

On Christmas day, the Polish band went door to door on St. Louis Avenue, around the Polish Falcons' Hall.

There was a trumpeter, a drummer, and an accordion player. They played Polish carols. The sounds of the bump, bump, bump of the drummer and accordion playing echoed up and down the street.

After the band played several carols at the door of 2205 St. Louis Avenue, Mr. Kosakowski would invite the musicians into the house for a drink. Usually, he served krupnick, a traditional drink made of simmering Vodka, dried fruit and honey.

An incident in the Blaskiewicz family of St. Hedwig Parish reflected both the loyalty of Poles to their adopted nation, and to their homeland. It made a powerful impression on young Jeanette and John Andrew Blaskiewicz, who were playing in their home at 4721 Minnesota Avenue when young John Andrew found family documents. The paperwork indicated that his family had emigrated from the part of Poland ruled by Russia. The youngster made an announcement. He said that their family were "Russian Pollacks." His father, a naturalized citizen, took his young son by the collar and pinned him against the wall. He told the young man that first of all they were Americans, and secondly they were of Polish descent.

Later, their father's bitterness toward the Russians was attributed to memories of cruel and degrading Russian domination of the Poles. The Blaskiewicz children were told that the Russians would tie Polish women to plows and use them as horses.

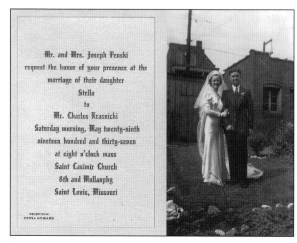

Mr. and Mrs. Joseph Penski request the honor of your presence at the marriage of their daughter
Stella
to
Mr. Charles Krasnicki
Saturday morning, May twenty-ninth nineteen hundred and thirty-seven at eight o'clock mass
Saint Casimir Church
8th and Mullanphy
Saint Louis, Missouri

RECEPTION: 2203A HOWARD

▲ After the wedding of Charles and Stella Krasnicki on May 29, 1937 at St. Casimir Church, the newlyweds posed on the lawn of their family's backyard at 2203 Howard Street. The photo documents that even the garages in North City featured decorative brick arches and glazed bricks. (Photo courtesy of Roger Krasnicki.)

During the 1930's, Polish St. Louisan, Walter "Sonny" Palkowski, was developing another persona as, "Sonny and his crying violin." While in North St. Louis, Sonny sang with the choir at Sts. Cyril and Methodius Church. Members of his church treasured his violin performances at Christmas Eve midnight mass.

On Saturday night, however, Sonny played Country music on Radio WEW with "Grandpappy Jones." He even cut a record.

Frank Gawlak, who had emigrated in 1917, had bought the four family flat at 1420 North 20th Street opposite St. Stanislaus. With consistent work hard to find, however, he was having trouble making the house payments. His children and their families, who were also living in the four family, were in the same circumstances. His son Julius, who then had his own family, was able to find some work on the wharves, carrying baskets of apples up the steep streets from the river. For this he was paid about fifty cents a day. With that, Julius was able to help his father make the payments on the flat.

Eventually Frank Gawlak became the caretaker and carpenter for St. Stanislaus Parish. He did a lot of the woodwork around the parish complex. Among his responsibilities was ringing the church bells three times a day. Also, he had to chase the pigeons out of the bell tower.

The job that created great consternation for his wife was washing the stained glass windows. The rose window on the facade of the church was particularly high. Gawlak would set an old wooden extension ladder on the steps, and brace it against the front wall of the church to reach the window. As he washed the window, his wife would be standing across the street, telling him he was going to fall and he was crazy for doing that.

With unemployment still so high that it was debilitating in almost every town and neighborhood across the United States, the threatening news from Europe seemed to fall on deaf ears. In what was called the Anschluss, Hitler's troops had marched into and claimed Austria. The United States Army could muster only 180,000 officers and men. The Navy numbered less than 114,000 men

◀ A class photo from St. Stanislaus Grade School taken in October of 1938. (Photo courtesy of Ray Gawlak.)

▲ A popular, Polish photo studio, the Buben Studio, took this 1938 wedding photo for the bride and groom, Genevieve Lubaszewski and Walter Zygmunt. (Photo courtesy of Bernice Krauze.)

▲ Sophie Kuberski Mindak selling fresh Wonder Bread at Mindak's Market at 25th and Howard Streets. Robert and Sophie Mindak opened their combination grocery and deli style restaurant and bar in 1937. Employees from nearby Samuel's Shoe Company and a plant of Brown Shoe ate Sophie's home-cooked lunches at the restaurant while her husband Robert tended the bar day and night. (Photo courtesy of Randy and Chris Mindak.)

and the Marines numbered 18,000. With a total defense establishment of little more than 300,000 men, America was little better off than in 1917.

On December 31, 1938, flames rushed through the Polish Falcons' Hall on St. Louis Avenue. Later, it was determined that a faulty flue had caused the conflagration. Whatever the cause, New Year's Day of 1939, after suffering through a whole decade of hardships, the Polish people of North City saw one of their social and cultural institutions in ruins.

Exhibiting great resilience, the Polish Falcons rebuilt their hall quickly. The upper floors were reconfigured as a combination gymn, dance hall and theatre. Where walls were destroyed, parlors were combined to serve as meeting rooms. Bits of the original decor that had survived the flames were maintained — a Victorian mantle, elaborate doorknobs, and ten foot tall pocket doors.

Soon the voices of Polish choirs, the sounds of children learning gymnastics, and polka melodies were reverberating through the Polish Falcons' Hall — with its Victorian remnants amidst its modern style amenities.

In the midst of economic hardships, the members of St. Hedwig Parish somehow managed to complete their sanctuary with the installation of stained glass windows in 1939.

Like most Americans, the Polish-Americans living around St. Stanislaus Church were worn by a full decade of economic depression that had stolen the savings of many, and the jobs of many more. With 19% of the workforce unemployed nationwide, family members who found jobs didn't dare to complain about the minimal salaries, dangerous conditions, or long hours. They were often responsible for putting food on the table for their parents, brothers, and sisters.

Even if they managed to save a little, Polish-American homeowners didn't consider adding modern plumbing, or other amenities to their homes. Employment was so uncertain that they felt the need to save that money. As a result, major work on homes was deferred and families continued to be dependent on outhouses for their plumbing.

Despite these hardships, the pride in and character of the Polish neighborhoods did not suffer. As a child, Raymond Gawlak watched as, "The Polish women in the neighborhood used to scrub the stone steps in front of their houses on their hands and knees. They also scrubbed the floor of St. Stanislaus Church on their hands and knees for all the holidays."

The news from Europe became ever more frightening. After marching into the Rhineland, taking over Austria and

▲ Brick rowhouses, with their shuttered windows and doors, pocket-sized front yards, brick sidewalks and picket fences, lined the streets around St. Stanislaus. (Photo courtesy of Ray Gawlak.)

Czechoslovakia, Hitler wanted Gdansk, the Polish port city on the Baltic. During the time Poland was divided, Gdansk was one of the cities controled by the Germans, and renamed Danzig. Hitler felt the city belonged to Germany and on August 19, 1939 demanded the Poles concede Gdansk. The Poles did not yield.

The World Erupts

Sixteen year-old Kazimierz Segieda was scheduled to report to the air force cadet school. He lived with his family in Kowel, in eastern Poland. At 5:00 in the morning, on Sunday, September 1, 1939, his whole family woke up to the sound of explosions — one, two, three explosions. The Segieda family had a battery-powered radio. "We turned it on to find out what was happening. They were announcing the Germans had declared war on Poland."

The earth-shaking explosions were caused by the bombing of the nearby railroad and bridge.

Hitler's Germany had begun pulverizing the airfields, roads, railways and civilian targets in Poland with a surprise attack by the Luftwaffe. Sixteen hundred marauding German Stukas, fighters and bombers began terror bombing Poland. These new airstrike tactics were designed as the first step in Hitler's new blitzkrieg, lightning war, that he would unleash across Europe.

▲ The news coming from Poland was too horrible to comprehend. Photos document that the Polish community of St. Louis continued to invest sweetness into their family and community lives, despite the hardships of the Depression, the evolving tragedy in Europe, and threats to the United States. Parishioners and parents went to great care to costume St. Stanislaus students like the trumpeter of Krakow for a play. (Photo courtesy of Ray Gawlak)

One hour after the Luftwaffe began dropping hell from the skies, the second step in this first use of blitzkrieg began. The fast-moving German Panzer tanks rolled into Poland — from north and south. The flat Polish plains provided easy surfaces for the tanks — and the dry, sunny September weather had hardened those plains, enabling the Panzer tanks to move even faster.

The Nazi invasion of Poland would knit the future of the Polish community of St. Louis with events and lives in Poland. Eventually, Poles like Kazimierz Segieda would survive the fascist invasions, to become one of the "displaced persons" who came to St. Louis to build new lives.

As a Boy Scout trained in emergency preparedness, Kazimierz Segieda had an assigned job in case of any disaster. That Sunday, during the attack, he proceeded to his mission. The 16 year-old went to his assigned road, which was packed with refugees. They were coming from the west, running from the Germans, to the safety of the east. In the midst of this chaos, the teenager served as a traffic cop giving directions.

The German Luftwaffe was destroying roads, railroads, bridges and trying to paralyze communications completely. It also bombed hospitals.

Hitler and Stalin had signed a secret pact that would cost Poland dearly. The Nazi-Soviet Non-Agggression Pact, signed on August 23, included plans to once again partition Poland. The pact resulted from a mutually cunning strategy on the part of the two dictators.

Hitler believed that Stalin would be satisfied with a large chunk of Eastern Poland, and stay out of the war until Germany was ready to invade Russia. Stalin saw the pact as a means of stemming Nazi aggression. But the speed of this new lightning warfare alarmed Stalin.

The Red Army invaded Poland on September 16th. Russian tank crews in Vilna told Polish civilians that they were on their way to fight the Germans. On September 18, however, the Russians met the Germans at Brest Litovsk and exchanged friendly greetings.

On September 25, the German-Russian agreement abolished the Polish state, carving it up between Germany and Russia. Two days later, Warsaw, ravaged by starvation, and pounded incessantly from the air, fell to the Germans.

The frightening news from their native land must have haunted the Polish immigrants in St. Louis. It seemed to many Poles in North City that their German neighbors were uncomfortable with, maybe even embarrassed by, the actions of the German state.

▲ With Hollywood fashions and an Art Deco style back drop, Anne Olander and Stanley Zygmunt's wedding photos in 1940 seemed thoroughly American. The bride had a large wedding party, since she had four sisters. The wedding took place at Our Lady of Czestochowa Church. (Photo courtesy of Bernice Krauze)

Genevieve Lubaszewski Zygmunt and her husband Walter Zygmunt followed the news from the apartment they rented at 1632 North 19th Street. They were some of the very few Poles living in their immediate neighborhood. The brutality in Europe reached their North St. Louis home in an ugly episode.

After the fall of Poland, Germans who lived on the block started throwing garbage into the Zygmunts' back yard. The bullies emptied the trash cans into the yard of the Polish immigrants, yelling "Ve Von the Var, Ve Von the Var."

The Russians closed all the schools in Eastern Poland, where Antoni and Petronella Kaminski lived. Their nine year-old son Adam began working full-time on the farm. Before the invasion, the Kaminski family had grown wheat, rye and corn for feed. Near the house, they tended a vegetable garden. They also raised pigs, cows, horses and lots of chickens.

"The Russians took our guns, we had no guns," Adam Kaminski recalled the early days of Russian occupation. As the environment became increasingly threatening to the locals, the farmers formed colonies.

Across the Atlantic, Americans were consumed with surviving the day-to-day challenge of putting food on the table. Jobs were scarce when Ben Walezak graduated from Central High School in 1940. He did find some clerical work, but needed more work.

Even though Walezak never went to a recruiting office, he met an U.S. Army recruiting Sergeant. He remembers being at a tavern when the Recruiting Sergeant gave him tokens for public transportation to take the young job hunter across town to Jefferson Barracks. On December 2, 1940, the day before Walezak turned 19, he took the streetcar to Jefferson Barracks and enlisted in the Army Air Corps.

In the Frenchtown neighborhood, Hager

Hinge Company, on Second Street, was a long time employer. People used to ask the students at Our Lady of Czestohova parish elementary school, "What do you intend to do (after graduation). Go to McKinley High School, or go to Hager Hinge College?"

Francisek Rudawski had always emphasized the importance of education to his family. In the fall of 1940, his son Joseph Rudawski began attending McKinley High School. Continuing his education, however, did not mean that he didn't need to help pay the family bills.

After school, young Joe Rudawski sold newspapers on the corner of South Broadway and Russell Boulevard. "I sold newspapers,

they cost 3 cents. For each newspaper sold, I was paid nine mills. There are 10 mills to a penny. Carfare, with a transfer, cost 10 cents," Rudawski related.

In Poland, the Red Army rounded up some 217,000 prisoners, notably army officers and middle-class intellectuals. The Russians rounded up any person they believed could potentially lead revolutionary efforts. They arrested Kazimierz Sugieda's father, because he was a forest ranger, and sent him to Siberia.

Both the Germans and the Russians were about to commence an unprescedented reign of terror on the Polish people.

In the midst of this devastation, Ben

▲ Charlie Krasnicki and his assistant at his first grocery store at 23rd and Warren Streets. Undaunted by the Great Depression, many Poles opened and operated small businesses. (Photo courtesy of Roger Krasnicki)

Krauze was born on January 1, 1940 in the town of Sobowka Rowne. The village numbered 50 to 100 families. Krauze's parents, like the other farmers, lived in the village, and farmed about 100 acres they owned outside the village.

The Germans forced the evacuation of the village. Mrs. Krauze would later describe the winter evacuation, "The wagon turned over in the snow, and we almost lost the baby."

While the Germans terrorized the Krauze family, the Segieda family was at the mercy of the Russians.

On February 10, 1940, "Russia takes my whole family to Siberia. I was 17 years, 10 days-old," Kazimierz Segieda stated. "My mother, three sisters, one niece are on the train to Siberia for 3 weeks. The cars are cattle cars. There is no toilet. We cut a hole in the floor for everybody, women, children, men, to use."

"There was no heat in the cars. The fortunate had a blanket."

"The Russians locked us in the car. We would progress twelve, 18 hours, then stop. Russians would open the car and ask if anybody was dead. Then throw out the bodies."

The food was brought to them in a barrel and shoveled onto the floor from the barrel. Russian fisherman, who fished with nets, had been paid by the barrel for their catch. There was as much rocks, dirt and snakes as fish in the barrels.

The train progressed. Through timber, through three feet of snow. It was 42 degrees below zero.

When the train came to its final stop in Siberia, there was another shock. "There was nothing. They gave us a shovel or axe, brought from some army store. We cut the timber. We built a shack, or we are dead. We built our own camp. I was 17 years old. I had the power to survive."

Once they were building their camp, "In Siberia, they delivered father to us, half dead. He only lived 6 or 7 months."

In the spring of 1940, the St. Louis *Post-Dispatch* reported the grim news from Poland. The Polish Government, operating in exile from Paris, had issued a book, "accusing Germany of trying to 'murder deliberately' the Polish fatherland." The Post Dispatch of April 2, 1940 carried assertions from the book, that the population in the German-occupied regions of Poland had decreased by 4,000,000 persons during the previous three months. According to the book, 604,321 prisoners and workmen had been deported to Germany. "…some 2,500,000 people who can be considered to have died as a result of war activities, executions, hunger, cold…"

"The Teutonic frenzy for destruction is above all directed against Polish public leaders," the book stated. "A sympton being the mass execution and deportation of Polish intellectuals."

It seemed to many Polish children and teenagers in St. Louis, that their parents, and uncles, and grandparents,… tried not to talk about what was happening in Poland. The children didn't hear the grown-ups discussing the horrifying news, not just from Poland, but from all of Europe. "Parents did not want to talk to children about these issues," Joe Rudawski explained.

businessmen in the neighborhood. Across the street was the Brockmeyer Cigar Company, a wholesaler for cigars, cigarettes and candy to the corner confectionaries. Brockmeyer also operated their own outlet shop on the corner.

When Rudawski was 15 and a half, he had to find more work. His dad was temporarily out of work at the car foundry and his mother had had appendicitis. The family needed to pay the bills from City Hospital. Teenaged Rudawski got a work permit. Mr. Brockmeyer hired him as a clerk on Saturdays and after school for 40 cents an hour.

As hard as life was, the tightly knit Polish communities added a sweetness to day-to-day existence.

Young Ray Gawlak was growing up in a three room apartment in the family's four

From his corner newspaper stand, Rudawski got to know the people and

◀ Virginia (left) and Genevieve Liszewski in the front yard of 925 Harlan Avenue in the Baden neighborhood of North City. (Photo courtesy of John and Donna Nachefski.)

▶ The wooden back porches, trellises, privacy fences and shrubs in the back yard of the their four-family flat on North 20th Street provided the setting for this photo of the Gawlak family. (Photo courtesy of Ray Gawlak.)

family flat across the street from St. Stanislaus. Frank Gawlak, the grandfather who had emigrated in 1917, owned the flat. He and his wife lived in one of the four units. Each of their three children, with their families lived in one of the units. Grandmother Antonette Gawlak edged all of the sidewalks in the back yard with brick. Her beds of purple Iris, with their sweet fragrance, bordered the walks. Rose of Sharon bushes, with their late summer blooms, were in the center of the yard. Privacy fences along the sides, and sheds and a garage in back gave the yard seclusion. Other neighbors' yards had brick patios and were enclosed, like courtyards. Around the courtyards they potted oleanders in big tubs. In winter time, the neighbors carried the oleanders to their basements, where they kept the tropical plants alive through the harsh winters.

Across the alley, an Italian produce vendor lived. He kept his horses in a stable at the back of his yard. Ray Gawlak would see him hitching up his horses to his trailer each morning to carry his fruit and vegetables up and down the streets to sell. Next to him was a lumber yard. A milkman also lived on the block. He delivered the milk by horse and wagon up and down the alleys. The neighbors used the horse droppings to fertilize their gardens.

Mr. Deptula, at 1402 North 20th Street,

used the manure to fertilize his front garden. There was only a small garden wedged between the brick sidewalks and the tall brick townhouse, with its shuttered windows. He tranformed that spot with an ornamental tree, and all sorts of flowers.

Since no one had air conditioning, in the evening, everbody would venture out on the street to cool off. Everyone knew each other. Long wood porches, and flights of wooden stairs, crisscrossed the backs of most of the flats. These two floors of porches, that usually extended the whole width of the houses, became havens in summer evenings. The Gawlak family, and often many of the neighbors, even slept on the porches, which caught every summer breeze.

At the summer picnic at St. Stanislaus, the men set up a portable dance floor on the playground. The picnic-goers danced a lot of polkas. In parish school, the children participated in plays. And the nuns taught the children to dance the Polish Kosac.

The quality of neighborhood life, however, could not protect

► A view of the two-story back porches from a back porch near St. Stanislaus Church. (Photo courtesy of Ray Gawlak.)

St. Louis Poles from the news from Europe.

St. Louis newspapers carried the news that Adolf Hitler had issued an edict calling for invasion of the U.S.S. R. on March 13, 1941. German troops drove into Russia along a wide front, from the Arctic to the Black Sea, on June 21, 1941.

The Polish government in exile, by then based in England, along with Churchill, proposed to Stalin that he release his Polish prisoners. The Poles, they urged, could increase the Allied Armies. With the Germans advancing, the Polish government in exile and the Russian ambassador in London came to an agreement about the future of Poles enslaved in the Soviet Union.

As a result, Kazimierz Segieda, along with many other young Polish men, joined the Polish Army in Russia on September 26, 1941.

The 18 year-old's father was dead and his family still working in timberland in Siberia.

These new Polish soldiers were soon stationed, "between Moscow and the Ural Mountains" Segieda stated. "We had no winter supplies, no uniforms. We were dieing like flies. They were supposed to move us to a warmer climate. They moved us to twelve miles from the Afghan border. We had no food, no medicine."

◄ Sergeant Stanley B. Rozanski, the son of Joseph and Antoinette Rozanski, was serving as a navigator aboard a B-24 Bomber that was shot down in North Africa on May 1, 1942. Nothing was recovered of the plane or crew. He was the first member of St. Stanislaus killed in action during World War II and the first St. Louisan killed in the Middle East campaign.

In Harm's Way

On December 6, 1941, Ben Walezak graduated from Chanute Field in Rantoul, Illinois, and headed back to St. Louis for a break. The next day, he and a girl friend walked to the neighborhood movie house. Walezak was wearing his U.S. Army uniform.

The movie stopped. The news flashed on the screen. The Japanese had attacked Pearl Harbor. There was quiet. Shock. Then another message came up on the screen, telling all military personnel to report to base.

It took a couple days for Walezak to arrange transportation to his next post, at West Soberfield, Massachusetts. There were tears in his Mom's eyes when he left.

Pearl Harbor further knitted together Poles in their native land with Polish Americans in St. Louis. The sons of the Polish American community of St. Louis would be scattered around the world, fighting to defeat the fascists regimes of Germany, Italy and Japan. Poles in their homeland struggled to somehow survive

▲ The cast members of the St. Hedwig Dramatic Club production of "Polski Uncle Sam."

the cruelties of both Germany and Russia.

Two members of Sts. Cyril and Methodius were among the American troops in the Pacific who were captured in those first months of the war. At the mercy of their brutal, Japanese captors, Henry Cichocki and Walter Piotrowski were two of the American POWs being deprived of water and food, often injured and beaten, and being forced on long marches through the tropical heat. They were victims of what became known as the Bataan Death March.

On the European front, Churchill recognized that the Poles at Stalin's mercy could, if fed, trained, and armed, play a significant role in the war. He continued to urge Stalin to increase supplies to the Poles. Eventually, Kazimierz Segieda and other young Poles were transported by train to the Caspian Sea. Then they traveled by boat to Iran, where, after much negotiating, Churchill succeeded in getting Stalin to release the Poles to the British.

The Poles were skeletons, wearing the same clothes-turned-to-rags that they had worn when they were taken to Siberia. Journalists witnessed and photographed the shocking image of these survivors of Stalin's wrath. There is no evidence of these photographs being published. But with Stalin then an ally of the United States, the story of

▲ Stanley Barlog, of the Kosciusko neighborhood, advertised War Bonds in the advertisements for his tavern on Menard and Barton Streets.

◀ William (Boleslaus) Nachefski sent this photo of himself, taken at infantry boot camp, home to his wife and daughter in South St. Louis City. He penciled, "I love you both so much," on the back of the photo. After the war, he refused to celebrate his birthday. This was a source of mystery to his children, until they learned that their uncle, William's brother, had been killed in action on his birthday. (Photo courtesy of John and Donna Nachefski.)

Kazimierz Segieda and the other Poles would not have helped morale back home in the United States.

Iran was heaven to these Poles. The English burned their rags. They disinfected the men. Segieda stated, "They let us shower, and shave. They fed us five times a day."

The British Army moved Kazimierz Segieda and his fellow Poles to Iraq for one year of training. Segieda became one of the five members of a tank crew of a Sherman tank. He served as the radio man and also fed artillery ammo to the gunner. His crew were members of the Polish 2nd Corps under the English command of General Montgomery, fighting with the American 5th Army.

Meanwhile, Ben Walezak trained at bases in the American West, then boarded the Queen Elizabeth Ocean liner, which had been transformed into a massive troop ship, in September of 1942. Walezak was headed for Thurleigh, England, where he would serve as a mechanic keeping American bombers over Germany. Walezak's older brother, Adam, became an infantryman. He was sent to Alaska, then threatened by the Japanese navy.

Mobilizing the nation for war was resulting in shortages. In response, the United States government began rationing meats and cheese on April 1. But the sacrifices for the war effort made by Americans at home were insignificant compared to the deprivation and cruelty suffered by Poles and Americans overseas.

By 1943, the situation for Polish farmers and their families had become extremely dangerous. To the Kaminski children, it seemed like open season on farmers. In addition to the Russian rule, there were now

German soldiers trying to kill farmers in the district that the Kaminski family called home.

"We hid on the farms at night," Adam Kaminski stated. One morning, the family found their father, Antoni Kaminski, in the field, shot. His whole face was blown off. "We don't know who killed him — partisans, Germans, Russians."

His widow and children went to town to seek safety. But there were, "too many people, no room, no food. Finally, we stayed in a convent, I think about two or three weeks. The nuns ran out of food too." Then, at end of

▶ Nazi guards took these photos of 13 year-old Adam Kaminski and his 20 year-old brother Stanley Kaminski when they were being shipped to slave labor camps in Germany. The guards stamped Stanley's photo with the Nazi swastika. (Photos courtesy of Adam and Stanley Kaminski.)

the summer of 1943, German troops rounded up the Poles who had taken refuge at the convent, put them on trucks, then on trains and sent them to Germany.

Adam Kaminski described what happened next. "At the border, we had to take all our clothes off. They sprayed us with powder and took our photos. There were two trains. One train goes to work camp. One train goes to gas chamber. We were lucky, we went to work camp."

Petronella Kaminski, her toddler-aged daughter, her daughter Maria, son Adam, twenty year-old son Stanley, and his wife and their one year-old son, went to the same work camp. Kaminski's daughter Helena was sent to be a farm laborer.

At the Camp, "We had to wear big 'P,' like the Jews had to wear Star of David. It was yellowish piece of cloth with white letter."

The camp was outside of a small German city with about 30,000 residents. The camp had been a sort of theatre hall or movie house. Inside the theatre, there were cages or cells, and the Kaminski family lived in one of those cages. This camp was about one and one/half miles from the factory where they worked. So each day, the workers walked to and from their work site.

At age 13 years, "I had to do work of a grown man," Adam Kaminski explained. He worked in a factory that made boxes for ammunition. He carried lumber up the stairs, and cleared the work sites around the machinery. At other times, he cut lumber - split dry wood for airplane wings. His mother was making bullets.

The enslaved Poles had only the clothes on their backs. "The guards gave us left over clothes from dead people, and used shoes from dead people. We wore them out," according to Kaminski.

"One time a day, in the evening, we ate." Kaminski described the food ration. The workers were allowed one piece of bread. "It was so thin, you could see through it. Soup, maybe a little carrot in it — sometimes it was just water. We'd steal potatoes, crab apples."

While the Kaminski family was trying desperately to survive, Kazimierz Segieda had restored his health,

▶ On September 20, 1943, young S.J. Trudzinski (a Frank Sinatra look alike) of St. Hedwig Parish died in the service of the United States.

was trained and was ready to fight. He and his Polish 2nd Corps, under General Anders, fighting with General Montgomery of the British 8th Army, were sent to Italy. They were to attack the "soft underbelly of Europe," defeating the fascist rule in Italy, and head for Germany.

The War had scattered young parishioners of St. Hedwig's Church around the globe. The names of 141 parishioners appeared in a list of members of St. Hedwig Church in uniform during 1944. The pastor's Christmas 1943 message from the parish and the Holy Name Society had reached parishioners serving in the jungle islands of the Pacific, and in the rainy cold of England. The homesick parishioners filled pages answering the letter.

"Tears of joy came to my eyes when I received your Christmas letter. It made me think of my good parents and the Midnight Masses I served in our St. Hedwig Church." Vincent Stolarski wrote to Father Zielinski. "Father I never thought I would miss my Pastor and my Parish the way I do ever since I came into the service," "But I'm praying to the Good God that this war will come to a victorious end soon, so that we can come home safely to our loved ones and to the Parish we all love so much."

John Jurkiewicz echoed Stolarski's thoughts, writing, "I really missed my parents and the Midnight Christmas Mass in St. Hedwig Church." Jurkiewicz noted, "…this was my first Christmas away from home."

Where ever the young parishioners were stationed, they treasured and shared the pastor's letter.

"Spend my Christmas with a nice English Family," Ray Wormek wrote the pastor. "I read your Christmas letter to them." Joseph Pijut penned, "Your Christmas letter made me happy." He must have read it to friends because he added, "My buddies liked it." Lieutenant M.T. Floryanski thanked Zielinski and the entire parish for offering Christmas Midnight Mass for parishioners in the service. He described it as, "the most cherished gift,…" Parishioner and serviceman James Winzen said Father's Christmas message, "really brought me cheer; it was like a star of heaven, piercing the fog of London."

First Lieutenant John Kulikowski wrote that he was serving with many men from the Eastern States, and among them are, "quite a few Polish boys. The Easterners think a lot of the Polish boys. They have not forgotten the valiant battle for Warsaw against the tremendous odds." His brother, Corporal Francis Kulikowski, looked forward to victory, to hearing the bells of St. Hedwig's ringing again, and to "praying as we never prayed before the war broke out." Their brother, Corporal Joseph Kulikowski, boasted that he had won, "my medal — sharp shooter — I am happy about it…" Their brother, Private Walter Kulikowski, had heard that "Stanley Trudzinski is missing….he is one of the Good Lord's heroes."

Casimir Kulikowski, Jr. confessed, "Well, Father, I have joined the Navy. I do not feel right in staying home while my four brothers are in the service. I, too, want to do my share for my Country."

On April 1, 1944, John Gruchala wrote to congratulate Father Zielinski on his Silver Jubilee. Then he told what he could of his own circumstances. "…am now in New Guinea. The weather here is very hot and close." He lamented that though, "Things are very interesting here," due to strict censorship, he could write very little.

"We have Mass every afternoon, and on Sunday mornings. I am going to make my Easter duty next Sunday."

"Please give my regards to my friends in the parish, and remember me to the Holy Name Society."

Only three weeks after writing that letter, on April 24, 1944, John Gruchala was killed in action on New Guinea.

In the Old North St. Louis neighborhood, Mrs. Walezak now was worried about another one of her sons. Young Walter Walezak had enlisted in the Army and was fighting his way through Italy.

Kazimierz Segieda was one of the thousands of Polish troops fighting in the Battle of Monte Cassino. Their goal was to break through the German lines to liberate Rome. The six month battle, beginning on January 4, 1944, left 350,000 men dead or wounded. Walter Walezak was awarded two bronze stars for his service in Italy.

While St. Louis Poles were fighting around the world, the aunts, uncles and young cousins of the Krauze family had been transported to Siberia, where half of them died. Their maternal grandfather and one of their uncles were killed in Dachau. The Krauzes were sent from one slave labor camp to another slave labor camp. At one of the camps, Mrs. Krauze worked in a hemp factory. Her deteriorated health and, evidently, something in the hemp caused a rash that was eating away the skin on one side of her face. A doctor at camp swore her to secrecy and gave her some sort of cream that healed her skin.

Later, the Krauze's young daughter Irene

scrounged some potato peels. She hid them in her blouse. "The gestapo lady caught her. She whipped her, slapped the living daylights out of her. Irene peed in her pants," according to her brother Ben.

Americans were bombing the camp, and the Krauze family, with all the other victims, ran out of the camp. "People were running into the woods," Ben Krauze described his earliest memory. "My father threw us into a ditch and covered us with his body. Some people were running back into the camp because they were trying to get some food from the kitchen. It was bombed, but they craved the food more than they feared the bombs."

Despite the rationing, shortages, and hardships caused by the War, life in the Polish neighborhoods of St. Louis was comforting, and still possessed a warmth.

Since Ray Gawlak lived almost in the

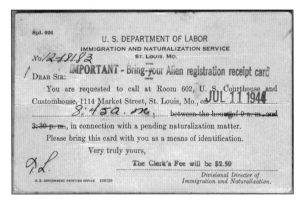

shadow of St. Stanislaus Church, he regularly served as an altar boy for the morning masses. Any morning the nuns found they were short an altar boy, they would run across the street and rouse Ray to substitute.

On Friday nights, toddler Thomas Bratkowski used to sit on the basement steps of his family's combination storefront and home in North St. Louis. His grandfather Henryk, a butcher, was slaughtering the chickens in the basement of his shop. Friday was a busy night because Saturday was the busiest shopping day. Young Thomas was afraid of the turkeys, because they were as tall as he was they might chase him.

On September 8, 1944, Joe Rudawski walked the two blocks from his family home on Victor Street to the streetcar stop at Broadway and Barton Street. There the eighteen year-old, who had graduated from McKinley High School that summer, boarded the streetcar and rode it through South City, and through South County, to the gates of Jefferson Barracks where he joined the United States Army.

After one week at Jefferson Barracks, Rudawski was shipped to Camp Fannin, Texas, for what was supposed to be 20 weeks of basic training.

◀ Like all immigrants, Joseph Naczewski was issued an alien registration card during the war. In July of 1944, only months before both his sons would be fighting in the Battle of the Bulge, he was ordered to the U.S. Courthouse concerning his pending "naturalization" to become an American.

On December 16, in a very costly attempt to reverse the Allied advance across Europe, the Nazi Armies staged a massive attack against the Allied lines. The German Armies pushed into the Allied lines, making a huge bulge into Belgium, surrounding Bastogne. The 101st Air Borne desperately held onto Bastogne. Thirty year-old Sgt. Stanley Kuszaj, of Our Lady of Czestochowa Parish, was killed on the Allied lines on December 20, 1944. Then Allied troops began the very costly advance, taking back yard, after yard of lost ground.

Both the Nachefski boys from St. Hedwig's Parish were threatened by this costly battle. Their parents at the two-family flat at 4707 Nebraska Avenue, in the Mount Pleasant neighborhood, did not know that their boys were fighting in Belgium only 20 miles apart from one another. On January 20, 1945, Philip Nachefski was serving with the Company B 509 Paratroopers. Along with his unit, he was dropped into a battle zone.

Maynard Pile, in the same unit,

◀ Philip Nachefski wore his paratrooper uniform for this movie star style photo. His family treasured the photo after Philip was killed in the Battle of the Bulge. (Photo courtesy of John and Donna Nachefski.)

was dropped with him. After he landed, Pile started for a ravine. He saw a German soldier on top of the ridge. Before he could get to the ravine, the German soldier shot him in the chest. The commanding officer ordered the paratroopers to leave Pile behind, he was too badly wounded.

Private Philip Nacheski, however, left the unit and came back for Pile. He dragged the wounded paratrooper through the ravine to a farm house, where a medic tent had been set up. Young Nachefski then returned to his unit.

Later that day, Philip Nachefski was killed in action. A month would pass before word would arrive at the Nachefski home that young Philip had been laid to rest in the First Army Cemetery in Belgium.

In the bitter winter weather, not just artillery and bullets wounded American soldiers. Frostbite cruelly disabled them. Afraid to further discourage civilians, the numbers of killed and wounded were not released to the American public. But recruits and their families were aware of something happening, because replacements were needed fast.

The United States Army could not wait for Rudawski and his buddies from Our Lady of Czestochowa — John Barlog, Eugene Krus and Albert Wania — to finish their basic training. They were pulled from Basic Training after only 18 weeks. They were given a three day furlough, spent at home.

The three buddies from the Polish neighborhood in Frenchtown, all graduates of Our Lady of Czestochowa, went to Baltimore by train. There they boarded the Queen Mary, an ocean liner packed with bunks to serve as a troop ship. After arriving in London, they boarded another troop boat to Le Havre. The ranking officers warned them to disregard it if the French acted cold to them in Le Havre. The officers explained that the Allied bombing of the port had caused the French city and its civilian population to suffer terribly.

In Le Havre, the three buddies, "boarded the forty & eights. They were old box cars. Each car held 40 people and had eight gauge tracks. They had bullet holes in them and were drafty." They rode the forty & eights for three days. The Polish buddies were only eighteen weeks of training from their old friends, and jobs, and school and church in St. Louis. And now they could hear the cannons and see the bombs bursting in the skies.

After the three days in the drafty box cars in that bitter cold winter, Rudawski broke down with pneumonia, and was sent back to the hospital. His friends were sent on — to what became known as the Battle of the Bulge.

Rudawski had double pneumonia, was spitting blood, and thought to have tuberculosis. After three weeks of recovery, he had been separated from his buddies, and the 4th Infantry was gone. "I was a person without a company, without a division." He stated, "There are soldiers walking around with parachute emblems on their hats. They put me in the 101st Airborne." Rudawski protested, "but I'm not a paratrooper." They answered, "Don't worry Joe, we'll put you in the Glider division, the 427th anti tank company. We'll train you."

Meanwhile, the German guards moved the Kaminski family to another camp, outside of another town. The Nazis had converted another movie house, by building cages in it to house about 250-300 enslaved workers. Here, the Kaminski family and other workers heard about some sort of uprising in Warsaw, from some of the 150 Polish women from Warsaw who were captured after the Uprising. After having been invaded by the Russians early in the war, it seemed strange to the Kaminski family that there were also seven Russians in this camp, who were prisoners like the Poles.

From this camp, the workers had to walk about twelve kilos each way to and from the factory. Kaminski remembered that along the route Hitler Youth and others would, "spit at us. They called us names, dirty names for

Jews and Poles."

The whole concept of time had changed for the teenage Adam Kaminski. Everyday they worked, with nothing to define weeks, or months. Only the changing weather, and bombs marked time. Since the family was forced to work in war plants, "We were bombed day and night. English bombed at daytime. Americans bombed at night. Like clockwork — noon and six in the evening."

"My mom cried a lot, she prayed all the time. My mom, she not ate too much, she gave it to the baby."

Even as an enslaved child, Adam Kaminski recognized there were, "good Germans and bad Germans." A mature German couple worked together at one of the machines in the factory. "Both their sons had died on the Eastern front — they were good people, they were good to me. They had a house, and some garden. They would make a sandwich for me and hide it in the lumber or stuff I had to clean up. If the Guards found them sneaking me food, they would have been punished."

News arrived at the Gawlak flat on 14th Street. Mrs. Frank Gawlak hung a gold star in the front window. Their youngest son, Eugene, had been killed in the Battle of the Bulge.

Joe Rudawski's promised "training" was his first ride on a glider.

The 101st Air Borne Division received many recruits because they had lost so many men. They were back up to divisional strength and moving into Germany. "Our Company was sent to Berchesgarten, Hitler's hide out by the Konig Sea. We were put in charge of guarding Goering's loot — all the artwork, emeralds, jewels. It was worth millions and millions of dollars. It was what Goering took from museums, from Jewish families, from the Nazis' victims."

Twenty-two year-old Corporal Frank Zero, of Our Lady of Czestochowa Parish, was killed on blood-soaked Okinawa on April 3, 1945.

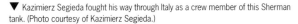

▼ Kazimierz Segieda fought his way through Italy as a crew member of this Sherman tank. (Photo courtesy of Kazimierz Segieda.)

On April 19, near Bologna, a German Panzer struck Kazimierz Segieda's Sherman tank. The driver was killed instantly, and the Sherman tank burst into flames. Segieda, his neck and shoulders burning, managed to get out of the hatch and jump from the tank. As he jumped, a German soldier shot him in the leg. Segieda would be hospitalized for four months.

Relentless Allied bombing was crumbling the German war machine. Nazi armies were retreating across Europe.

Then, 14 year-old Adam Kaminski saw the German soldiers and guards pull out of the work camp. It was in the spring of 1945. For the first time in six years, the young boy was able to celebrate. He, his family and fellow prisoners went out, into the street. They could see the Americans coming in. At the sight of the Americans, they were screaming and hollering.

After about a week passed, there were lots of American soldiers and many of them could speak German, Italian or Polish. "We saw a lot of the soldiers," Kaminski recalled. "We had more fun with the American soldiers."

Looking at the starving workers, and their cages, "the soldiers knew what had happened to us." Having witnessed these crimes, the American soldiers tried to seek out some kind of justice.

The Americans, "gave us guns. They asked, 'what do you want to do?'"

The soldiers put malnourished, 14 year-old Kaminski in their jeep. Then they drove down the street that the boy used to walk along to go to the factory — often being spat at and called names along the route. So they drove that street and Adam shot out the windows on one side of the street. Then they drove back and Adam shot out the windows on the other side.

When he got back to his mother, however, and she learned what he had done, she "beat the hell out of me." The woman who had seen her family enslaved and starved by Germans kept saying over and over, "you don't want to be like the Germans, you don't want to be like them."

The Nazis may have been defeated, and the war in Europe over, but war still raged in the Pacific.

Rudawski's company joined a division, moving back through France, heading to the port at Le Havre. "The 101st was deactivated and we became the 82 nd Airborne. We were heading to the Far East," to fight the Japanese.

Meanwhile, President Harry S. Truman brought the ongoing carnage in the Pacific to a sudden end, by ordering the dropping of the atomic bombs.

When Rudawski arrived at Le Havre, "We were informed that Japan had surrendered. I was feeling in good spirits. Just about everybody got drunk."

The company spent two weeks in London, then boarded the Queen Mary to return to the United States. "The Queen Mary had been equipped to handle the maximum number of troops," Rudawski said. "The bunk beds were stacked high." His was in the former swimming pool. "The aisles between the high stacks of bunks were so narrow that only one soldier could walk the aisle."

On the trip home, there were 60 mile an hour gales, making Rudawski feel sea sick. He decided to get some air. "I walked to a railing to get some fresh air and saw a soldier at the rail." It was Eugene Krus, his buddy from Our Lady of Czestochowa, McKinley High School, and the neighborhood. Since he was still in the 4th infantry, Rudawski asked about the other guys.

Albert Wania had been transferred, so Krus didn't know his whereabouts. But he told Rudawski the fate of their buddy John Barlog. The first day Barlog arrived at the front lines in the Battle of the Bulge, he was killed by German machine gun fire.

When the Queen Mary arrived in New York, "Everybody ran to the deck to see the Statue of Liberty. When we docked, Rosemary Clooney was singing to us. We felt good."

Ben Walezak left England on August 30, 1945. The trip to England three years earlier had taken five days on the Queen Elizabeth. The trip home was on a "little old dinky ship, a liberty ship called the SS Marshall Elliott." The voyage to New Jersey took two long weeks. Then he took the train to Jefferson Barracks, where his sister and niece picked him up after he was discharged. They brought him home.

As he walked into the family home on Sullivan Avenue, his mother was sitting in the kitchen, looking out the back window. When she turned and saw her Ben, her eyes flooded. In Polish she said, "Oh my darling son."

Several weeks later, Ben Walezak saw his old friend Walter Piotrowski at a neighborhood gathering. Piotrowski told the fate of their friend and fellow parishioner of Sts. Cyril and Methodius. Both Piotrowski and Henry Cichocki had been prisoners on the Bataan Death March. Henry Cichocki had died while they were on a POW ship heading for Japan, and had been buried at sea.

Peace

The women around St. Stanislaus would scrub the stone front steps of their homes with Bon Ami. It was their job to keep the stones white, and the neighborhood nice. If a neighbor didn't get the steps scrubbed, another neighbor would let her know that she had not done her job.

The old Polish neighborhoods of North City, with their brick sidewalks, gleaming white steps, Victorian row houses, courtyards, neighborhood playgrounds, corner shops and taverns — were a welcome site to the returning veterans.

As the neighborhoods had helped people survive the hardships of the Depression and World War II, now they would provide a setting for people to rebuild their lives. Here they would reconnect with old friends and organizations while starting new jobs. The children in the neighborhoods would delight in the color, character and freedoms the communities offered. These neighborhoods would also provide a

▶ Young Ray Gawlak on the sidewalk of North 20th Street, near St. Stanislaus Church. The furniture company in the background employed many Poles throughout its history. (Photo courtesy of Ray Gawlak.)

wholesome setting for new Americans, survivors of slave labor camps, in their desperate struggle to rebuild their shattered lives.

Ray Gawlak remembered Polish families living up and down the St. Stanislaus church block. Across the alley, were more Polish families and Italian families.

On summer days, a cart came down the street, selling flavored shaved ice, and candied apples.

The teenagers could walk to Sportsman's' Park to see the Cardinals play. They walked

Joseph Naczewski officially became a Citizen of the United States of America on November 2, 1945, eleven months after his son Philip had been killed in action. The government clerk filling out the naturalization forms incorrectly spelled his name as "Nachefski," forever changing the spelling of the family name. (Documents courtesy of John and Donna Nachefski.)

◄ A summer scene on the grounds of St. Stanislaus Parish. (Photo courtesy of Ray Gawlak.)

to local movie houses, and they walked, sometimes took a streetcar, to go Downtown. "Everybody knew each other. And everybody got along. It was a good neighborhood," Ray Gawlak stated.

At the end of the war, the Bratkowski family moved from their two room apartment attached to the grandfather's butcher shop, at 4200 North 11th Street in Hyde Park, to their own home. John and Elsie Bratkowski bought a 19th century four-family flat at 1215 -17 Hebert Street. The family of four, and soon family of five, occupied a four room unit on the first floor, while renting the other units.

The old outhouses still stood in the backyard of their Victorian era home on Hebert. John Bratkowski knocked them down to make way for a new garage. When they first moved in, the home was a cold water flat. Elsie heated the water on the stove for the family baths. The baby was bathed in the kitchen sink. Everyone else bathed in a metal tub that John carried up from the basement. On Saturday night, during bath time, the radio aired the "Uncle Dick Slack" show, with his popular tunes, or the Grand Ole Opry.

Social life revolved around the Polish Falcons Hall on St. Louis Avenue. On Friday evenings, the young folks and young men returning from the service gathered in the big meeting room on the first floor of the hall. There they informally gathered around the old upright piano and sang.

The Falcons choir numbered 60 members. The members studied and performed Polish songs, plus a few American tunes.

In summer time, dancing under the stars was a favorite activity. Volunteers set up the portable, wooden dance floor in the Falcons', big back yard. The members would polka, waltz and and swing until midnight, or 1:00 a.m. Then they would find the energy to dismantle the wood dance floor, and store it under the stage.

In addition to dances and singing, the Falcons' meetings were held on some Friday nights. It was at one of these Friday night meetings that Mary Sendobry noticed one of the young men who had just returned from the service. Mary couldn't find anyone to introduce her to the young man. Determined to catch his attention, she pricked Ted Sulzer with a hat pin. The hat pin worked. The two fell in love and were married on October 22, 1949 at St. Adalbert Polish Roman Catholic Church.

Since 1944, Joseph Penski had worked at the American Foundry on St. Louis Avenue near Broadway. Penski, who was born in 1889, would scrape and clean out the furnaces in which iron was melted for castings. The furnaces were extremely hot, especially the

floors. The workmen had no protective shoes.

Every workday, Penski got up at 5:30 a.m. At the family home at 23rd and Warren Streets, his wife Mary would bathe his feet. The skin on his feet was fragile, and broken from being in intense heat. The Penskis had gotten a special salve from the doctor. Mary would carefully spread the salve all over Joseph's feet, then wrap them in bandages.

After a breakfast of coffee and toast, Joseph Penski walked over a mile to the foundry, never complaining.

The paratrooper whom Philip Nachefski had saved in the Battle of the Bulge, Maynard Pile, paid a visit to St. Louis while on his honeymoon. He had a picture of Philip Nachefski, with the address 4707 Nebraska Avenue on the back. He went to the home, where he met Philip's mother. She spoke very little English, so her daughter-in-law translated for him.

After recovering from the burns and bullet wound in Italy, Kazimierz Segieda had returned to his company. He had spent a year in Italy, before being transferred to England. There he went to school for six months in a machine shop. In 1948, he was discharged. "They tell me, 'now you are free.'" He remembered, "I was a citizen without a country." He was not alone in his predicament. According to Segieda, "There were a quarter million Polish soldiers in England."

When the war ended, the Krauze family lived in Displaced Persons (DPs) camps, run by Americans. The barracks, "were big rooms. Depending on the size of the rooms, there were 20 to 30 families in each room," Ben Krauze recalled. "With blanket partitions between the families."

"At the DP camps, people were all mixed up. There were Ukrainians, Russians and Czechs." After the war, in the DP camp, Krauze remembered that his family, "had a sense of hope." Relatives still in Poland wrote to the Krauze family in the camp, "don't come back to Poland. Things are very bad. There are no jobs, no places to live."

In 1949, while still in a DP camp, the Krauze family received their papers to come to the United States.

The Krauze family not only had no money, but they had to face the housing shortage in the United States, and specifically in St. Louis. Their first four months in St. Louis, the family of four lived in two rooms of a four room unit in a two family flat. They shared the bathroom with another family. The flat was on St. Louis Avenue, near Sacred Heart Parish.

"My Mom worked at General Paper Stock Company on 7th Street."

"It was a dirty job. There was a conveyer belt with used paper on it. She sorted paper to recycle it," according to Ben Krauze. His father found work at a furniture company at 20th Street and Cass Avenue. After it closed, he washed dishes at Forum Cafeteria, near Famous and Barr.

"My father paid back Catholic charities for the boat fare to America. He paid back every penny, as soon as possible. He didn't want that debt hanging over him." Krauze explained that any short term aid the family received was in the form of a loan, that had to be repaid. Along with repaying the boat fare, the Krauze family also had to make tuition payments at St. Stanislaus School.

Though they were nine and 14 years-old, Ben and Irene Krauze had to start in kindergarten. "We had to learn our ABCs."

At the same time, the Kaminski family had been transferred from one DP camp to another DP camp since the war had ended. "American organizations delivered food, clothes and shoes. We stood in line for them," according to Adam Kaminski. "Every week the food was better."

Petronella Kaminski walking along the brick sidewalks of North St. Louis City, where she rebuilt her life after surviving Nazi work camps. (Photo courtesy of Maria Baras.)

► After the war, Maria Kaminski met Konstanty Baras in a displaced persons camp. They married and had two children before they emigrated and settled in North St. Louis City. At Buben Studio, they posed for this family photo in front of the backdrop that Polish immigrants had posed in front of thirty years earlier. (Photo courtesy of Maria Baras.)

The Kaminski family was in Germany the whole time. "At one point the Russians took us." But the Kaminski family made their way back to the American Zone.

Mary Kaminski married a Ukrainian man she met in one of the camps, Konstanty Baras. They were able to come to the United States, and settled in St. Louis. Mary, her husband, and their two young children lived in an alley house without indoor plumbing, on 14th Street, just north of Cass Avenue.

Young Adam Kaminski, still in Europe, joined the newly organized Polish Army working for the United States Army. In 1950, Adam, his mother Petronella, and two sisters were also allowed to immigrate to the United States. When they arrived, they moved in with Maria and her family, in the three room alley house dependent on an outhouse.

Adam got a job washing dishes at Forum Cafeteria in Downtown St. Louis. Soon he was organizing soccer teams for the local chapter of the Polish National Alliance.

Roger Krasnicki was growing up over his father's grocery store at 2300 Warren Street in the Old North St. Louis neighborhood. There was a mix of people in that neighborhood including Poles, Germans and Italians. Jewish families had a dry cleaners and a hardware store. "We all got along very well."

On Saturdays, Kasnicki's grandfather Penski walked to the Polish Hall where he and his buddies enjoyed a beer and played pinochle. At noon on Sunday afternoons, the whole house had to be quiet. It was time to listen to the Polish radio show aired lived from the Broadview Hotel in East St. Louis on WTMV. A recording of Chopin's Military Polonaise introduced the all-Polish radio show.

If the Deptula family opened their front door at 1402 North 20th Street, and opened the door of St. Stanislaus Church, the family could see from their living room through the church to the altar. So when John Stygar wanted to provide limousine service to take Eleanor Deptula across the street to marry Stanley Podolski, she refused. She was afraid she would wrinkle her dress getting in and out of the limo. So, on September 4, 1950, dressed in a flowing, white gown, Eleanor picked up her satin train and marched across the street, then laid down her train and walked up the aisle.

John Bratkowski was determined that his family have their own bath in their home on Hebert Street. About 1950, he was able to install hot water. He replaced the old copper tub in the basement with a cast iron tub. Two years later he added a full bath on the first floor and a full bath in one of the rental units.

Tom Bratkowski played in the school yard of nearby Ames School and in Strodtman Park, a neighborhood park and field just north of their home on Hebert. "We played softball and basketball in the school yard."

"The field sports were in Strodtman Park. And summer craft programs. The summer program was like a well-organized day camp that began as soon as school let out. Students from Harris Teachers' College organized the program."

"There was a wading pool in Strodtman Park. It was only a foot or so deep. The first Saturday after school let out was a disappointment. But the first Monday, word went out through the neighborhood, 'They're filling the pool.'"

Several times a week, park staff showed movies in Strodtman Park. "They put up a big screen. It was tied to a tether ball post to secure it. Kids brought blankets to sit on. Sometimes the popcorn man came by and cashed in on the movies.

"They showed the Laurel and Hardy series. They ran the movies several times. People watched. There was no TV."

▲ Kazimierz Segeida, far left, at a party of Polish veterans in Manchester, England, taken on March, 15, 1951, the night before his immigration to the United States.

In 1951, Kazimierz Segieda came to the United States. Truman had given refuge to a percentage of the Polish veterans. Segieda was crossing the United States when he ran out of money — in St. Louis. He got a job at the American Car Foundry on Broadway. After it flooded, he went to work for the railroad.

Throwing Out the Baby with the Bath Water

▲ Maria Baras and children in their back yard at 1847 North Market. Privacy fences sided the yard and outhouses were in the back. (Photo courtesy of the Baras family.)

eople moving from small towns to work in factories, veterans returning home, new immigrants, and the baby-boomers made most St. Louis neighborhoods — including the Polish neighborhoods — overcrowded. The housing shortage was affecting life not just in St. Louis, but in cities across the nation. St. Louis neighborhoods, however, had another problem — a plumbing shortage.

The City had experienced a tremendous building boom during the Victorian era. That boom had left the City with a wealth of Victorian housing that had been built before indoor plumbing.

Many of the 19th century homes had been updated, with full baths added in the 1920's. But the economic hardships and uncertainties of the Great Depression had brought a halt to luxuries like updating homes. Then the shortages for the war effort did not allow for adding amenities to homes. When the City Plan Commission reviewed the status of St. Louis' housing in 1947, they determined that 33,000 dwellings still had out houses.

In the neighborhoods around St. Stanislaus Kostka Church and around St. Casimir Church, 60 to 70 % of the dwelling units were dependent on outside toilets. Around Our Lady of Czestochowa, 70 to 80% of the dwellings had outdoor privies.

This sanitation problem, which profoundly affected the quality of life, had to be addressed. Unfortunately, the proposed solution was not to encourage the installation of modern plumbing.

Civic leaders in St. Louis, and across the nation, proposed fixing the housing shortage, eliminating the plumbing shortage, and correcting social ills, by demolishing old neighborhoods. The already historic areas of St. Stanislaus Parish and St. Casimir Parish were seen as "obsolete." While Polish St. Louisans were rebuilding their lives, their families, and their careers and while veterans were reconnecting with their neighborhoods, plans were in process to erase those neighborhoods.

On January 17, 1950, the Federal Housing Administration officially told the St. Louis Housing Authority to develop detailed plans for low rent housing on the near north side.

The proposal was to demolish all the building stock in an enormous part of the near north side, including everything around St. Stanislaus Parish on North 20th Street. In place of the historic neighborhoods, 2,490 federally subsidized units and 750 privately financed units would be built. The housing projects would cover a 180-acre tract, bounded by 18th Street on the east, Jefferson Avenue on the west, Franklin Avenue (later renamed Dr. Martin Luther King Boulevard) on the south and Cass Avenue on the north. The proposed public housing was designated the DeSoto-Carr housing project.

By December of 1951, the *Globe-Democrat* was reporting on the opening of bids on construction for the first of three housing projects planned for the site encompassing this huge area. The first component was the Captain Oliver Wendell Pruitt Apartments, 11 stories high, brick and reinforced concrete buildings with 1,736 dwelling units.

At this time, public housing was segregated, and the Pruitt apartments, covering only 26 of the 180 acres, was planned to, "accommodate about 6,900 Negroes," the *Globe-Democrat* reported. This project, named to honor a St. Louis African-American pilot killed in World War II, bordered the west side of the parish block, and stretched west to Jefferson. Adjoining acreage was set aside for more high rise projects, the William L. Igoe Apartments, designed to house 1,050 White families.

The *Post-Dispatch* reported, on April 25, 1952, that the site, "has been almost entirely cleared of the old slum structures, and a

▲ Andrea Krasnicki's first communion photo was taken in front her her father's grocery, "Charlie's Market." (Photo courtesy of Roger Krasnicki.)

▲ Barbara McCarty with her arms around her brothers Charlie and Tom at the St. Stanislaus picnic of 1953. Their father was Irish and their maternal grandparents were Teofil and Teofilia Chrostowski. (Photo courtesy of Linda Lawson.)

contract has just been let for demolishing the few remaining old buildings."

The commissioner of the Public Housing Administration toured the construction site in the fall of 1953 and declared himself impressed by the way the project was pushing, "into the skyline to replace a jumble of slum dwellings." He also announced more funding for more projects.

The resulting Pruitt-Igoe housing project consisted of 33 high rise structures, with approximately 2,700 units, on a 57-acre parcel of land.

In 1954, the *Globe-Democrat* reported the "razing of another slum area," had begun on August 20. It was the final section of the "huge DeSoto-Car public housing development…

consisting of Wendell Pruitt Homes, William L. Igoe Apartments and the yet unnamed Missouri 1-6, to have 4,186 low-rent homes in an area bounded by Carr, Cass, Eighteenth and Twentieth streets."

The hoopla, the articles of praise, and the speeches about these great new housing projects did not consider the cost.

The whole block across from the church was, "condemned" to make way for the last phase of the housing projects. It broke Mr. Deptula's heart to lose his home. The old Polish Hall, the site of thousands of Saturday afternoon pinochle games and of Saturday evening wedding receptions, was razed for this housing project. The Central Funeral Home, where many Poles had said goodbye to their loved ones, and the large Jewish Market so popular with the Poles, Gershon's, were demolished. With its Polish neighborhood leveled and scattered, the Polish weekly newspaper of St. Louis ceased publication. Networks of neighbors, lifelong friends, and neighborhood businesses were decimated.

With this final phase, later known as the Vaughn Apartments, the old neighborhood built by Polish parishioners of St. Stanislaus around their church was gone. Their community was scattered.

The growth of industry along North Broadway, especially during the War, had encroached on the parish territory of St. Casimir. The parish, however, still boasted 700 members. The parishioners operated eight societies including a sewing circle, sports club and charitable society. Branches of the Polish Roman Catholic Union, a Polish society and the Polish American Relief Society were among the clubs and organizations meeting in the parish hall. The parish was financially sound, its income exceeding its expenses by more than 30%.

The majority of "our old people have never learned the American language," according to the pastor of St. Casimir, Father Vincent Mogelnicki. "We still preach, read the announcements, and the gospel in

▲ Though their neighborhood had been taken by eminent domain and was being demolished, the members of St. Stanislaus Kostka Parish continued with their traditions. The girls of the parish wore their finery to take part in the May Day procession of 1955.

Polish… and our confessions are 95% Polish," Mogelnicki wrote in 1954.

In March of that year, the parishioners and pastor were shocked to see the proposed route of the Mark Twain Expressway (Interstate 70), published in community papers. The route of the new Interstate highway "goes right through our Church." The pastor wrote that his parishioners, "asked me to protest immediately this routing."

In a letter to Archbishop Ritter, dated March 16, 1954, Father Mogelnicki referred to "…the resentment felt by the Poles of the City over the fact that two of their parishes — St. Hedwig's and St. Adalbert's — have been Americanized. They frankly acknowledge that this would happen eventually but they cannot understand why the process should be rushed."

Mogelnicki also stated that his

▲ After the May Day procession in 1955, young ladies posed in front of the altar. (Photo courtesy of Linda Lawson.)

parishioners,…"are very much aware of the constant clash between the Germanic and Polish peoples, and since Your Excellency is of German descent they point to this factor as influencing the line of conduct you are following in eliminating the Polish parishes of the city….In fact at practically every meeting we hold where this matter is broached one or other of the old-timers will get the floor and before he is through he will be strongly declaiming about German domination, and that he for one will refuse to be Hitlerized,…"

In seeking Ritter's help to save the Polish parish, Mogelnicki stated, "…I have been making some inquiries via the telephone to the Missouri State Highway Office in Clayton and from their comments

▶ The 1957 Princess Dance was an excuse for the Polish Falcons to don their formals and celebrate life. (Photo courtesy of the Polish Falcons Nest 45.)

I have gathered the impression that they ordinarily do not route roads through Church property except with the consent of the church authorities involved." Despite pleas and protests by the parishioners, the Polish church was not spared.

The swath cut through North City for Interstate 70 took St. Casimir Parish. The Missouri Highway Department paid the Archdiocese $182,500 for the St. Casimir Parish properties in 1956. Another $137,500 was paid for the church and rectory of nearby St. Michael parish, the historic Irish parish founded in 1849.

Henryk Bratkowski's Polish butcher shop was also in the path of Interstate 70. After it was razed, Henryk moved in with his son John and daughter-in-law Elsie on Hebert Street.

The future of Our Lady of Czestochowa

▲ The Polish Hall on St. Louis Avenue was a popular site for wedding receptions. After marrying Ray Pestka, Pat McCarty threw her bouquet to the anxious young ladies in the Falcons Hall, on October 18, 1958. (Photo courtesy of Linda Lawson.)

Parish in Frenchtown was also dimming. In this case, the end was more natural. The Parish had been founded in 1907 to serve the immigrants settling near and among the industries in the oldest part of Frenchtown, east of Broadway along the river and railroad tracks. Their numbers had grown to the point that Kosciusko became the official name for that part of Frenchtown, between the river and the Soulard neighborhood.

The growth of the industry and their needs for space, however, were gradually diminishing the residential character of the area. The neighborhood and industry were becoming less and less compatible. One at a time, paying market rate, the industries were buying the homes of Polish-Americans.

After years of renting, and with his Kosciusko neighborhood shrinking, Francisek Rudawski decided that it was time for a change. He bought a home for his family in the Shaw neighborhood, next to the Missouri Botanical Garden and Tower Grove Park. Rudawski, however, never moved into the new home. He died suddenly. It was learned that he had had a heart condition, that was particularly stressed by his physical work in the extreme temperatures of the foundry.

At his urging, his son Joe had gone to college and graduate school on the Gl bill and was now teaching high school.

By 1957, Our Lady of Czestochowa parish had served three generations of Polish-Americans. The church was filled to overflowing for the last mass on Sunday, October 27. Many people unable to get seats stood on the steps leading into the church.

After the church was closed, and the altars and pews removed, "There was a brief respite before the wreckers came," Henry Tucholski wrote. "Some of us have lived all our lives in this old neighborhood. We were accustomed to seeing Czestochowa Church day after day, for so many long years. Many of us had attended the little two-room school. Therefore, it saddened us - those of us more sentimentally inclined when the wreckers finally came on December 10th."

The area around St. Adalbert Parish in Walnut Park was one of the few city neighborhoods with a substantial number of vacant lots available at the end of World War II. Brick homes and frame homes, some variations of ranch style, were constructed in the community during the post-war housing boom. Some Polish families, displaced by the demolition for Pruitt-Igoe and Interstate-70, were able to build or buy here. With the community growing, St. Adalbert's parishioners built a new, larger, contemporary-style church facing Woodland and Wren Avenues. The parish complex — with church, rectory and school — created a charming focal point for the small, friendly, Polish neighborhood.

The other Polish neighborhood that still had room to grow circled St. Hedwig Parish. When the stock market crashed in 1929, stunting investing and building across the nation, vacant lots still dotted the Mount Pleasant neighborhood. When the veterans came home from World War II, new yellow and orange brick houses were built on side lots and on scattered empty parcels around the area. The parish, though officially no longer an ethnic church, was still spiritual home to the surrounding Polish community. These new houses became homes to the next generation of the Polish community in the neighborhood. The parish was growing, and the combination church and school building from 1904-7 was overflowing.

▶ An architectural detail from the strikingly modern St. Hedwig Church. (Photo by Sheila M. Harris.)

St. Hedwig's parishioners hired an architect from northern Indiana, J.T. Golabowski, to design an extraordinary contemporary church for the little Polish parish. Members of the parish walked door to door collecting donations. They raised the $350,000 required to build the new church.

The new St. Hedwig Church, arguably one of the finest works of modern architecture in St. Louis, faced the corner of Itaska Street and Compton Avenue at an angle. The corner itself was treated as a small, five-sided plaza, framed by streets, the facade of the church, and small flower beds. The decorative features of the church — both on the facade and the interior — were carried out in sleek, modern lines and contemporary materials. Aluminum mullions created patterns in the stained glass. Rectangular shapes, no gothic arches, accentuated the design.

The interior of the church, unlike traditional naves, was fan-shaped. The church felt cozy, while seating 500. With its brick and marble walls, terrazzo floors, aluminum and brass railings, and light transformed by hidden stained glass — the effect of the interior was breathtaking.

In 1959, the *Post-Dispatch* sports page was regularly reporting the achievements of, "The Polish Falcon athlete," Wanda Wejzgrowicz. On Sunday, June 7, a *Post-Dispatch* article reported that Wejzgrowicz, who had finished third in the National A.A.U. competition the previous year, had broken her own record. A field and track star who bowled in winter, Wejzgrowicz often competed in the discus throw and shot put. At the annual Ozark A.A.U. women's track and field competition held at Francis Field, she bested her own record by two inches, heaving the shot 38 feet 10 and 1/2 inches.

In 1960, growing St. Adalbert Parish in Walnut Park constructed an additional school building to accommodate their children.

▲ Wanda Wejzgrowicz, of the St. Louis Chapter of the Polish Falcons Nest 45, placed Third in the shot put competition in the Pan American Games of 1959. (Photo courtesy of Wanda Wejzgrowicz.)

Rebuilding, Again

By the 1960's, the original Polish neighborhoods were history. The taking of huge sections of North City by eminent domain for housing projects and the construction of Interstate-70 had scattered Polish Americans. Using loans for new housing available through the GI Bill, many bought new homes in nearby North St. Louis County. Redlining and block busting tactics had caused housing prices on many more blocks on the near north side of the City to drop, even plummet. As a result, more young Polish-American couples settled in North County communities.

Though many Poles had been uprooted, they still gathered at their churches to absorb the changes in their lives and in the world.

When President John F. Kennedy was assassinated, the pastor of Sts. Cyril and Methodius Church performed a mock funeral for the President. He felt some embodiment of the President was needed so people would

▲ The Polish Falcons bowlers lined up at the Northland Bowl during their 1959-60 season. (Photo courtesy of the Polish Falcons Nest 45.)

have something to see. A casket was set in the front of the church. On each side of the casket, candles were placed — the tall, black candlesticks used at funerals. There was incense, and a full funeral mass. About a hundred parishioners attended.

The same gang Ben Walezak knew from growing up in Old North St. Louis played cards on Saturday nights at their homes. Gradually, more and more of their card games

▲ Polish Falcons Agnes Podolski, Dolores Sokolowski, Mary Sulzer, Lottie Gawendzinski, and Helen Bachuzewski. (Photo courtesy of the Polish Falcons Nest 45.)

▲ Stanley Krauze, Maria Baras, Petronella Kaminski, an unidentified friend, Helen Kaminski Kirkiewicz, and Paulina Krauze lined up on a bench in the school yard during the parish picnic in 1969. The walls of the Pruitt-Igoe housing complex, which shadowed the parish, can be seen above the fencing in the background. (Photo courtesy of Maria Baras.)

were being played in North County.

An old truism that South St. Louisans used to say about North City, now applied to North County. If you attend a wedding reception on the North Side, "expect to see some good dancing." South Side Germans marveled at the Poles' polka and swing dancing.

Ray Zielinski was elected the Mayor of the North County municipality of Bellefontaine Neighbors in 1963. He would hold that post for twelve years.

The Pruitt-Igoe housing projects, adjacent to St. Stanislaus, had festered with crime almost from their opening. By the 1960's, they were notoriously crime-ridden. The parish board asked the St. Louis Archdiocese to lend the parish the money to repair the bullet-pocked roof and the windows of their church. The Archdiocese had provided many loans to new suburban parishes to construct new buildings. There was even an annual collection from existing parishes earmarked to subsidize new parishes. St. Stanislaus Parish, however, was denied a loan. Somehow, the struggling board and parishioners managed to do the emergency repairs.

In 1969, Joe Rudawski, by then a school principal, became active with the parish. The parish funds were depleted. He recalled that he and fellow member of the Board of Directors, Mitchel Jeglijewski, built the parish bank account by taking their CDs and running from one bank to the next to, "see if we could beat the rate by a quarter of a percent." Eventually, the parish was getting up to 13% interest on their CDs. Then Rudawski and Jeglijewski began investing in stocks, that weren't volatile, and in bonds.

A powerful voice from the homeland visited the members of St. Stanislaus Parish on August 26, 1969. Archbishop Karol Wojtyla, the Archbishop of Cracow, came to St. Louis. After a visit with the Cardinal of the St. Louis Archdiocese, John Carberry, and touring the city, he went to St. Stanislaus. He spent hours at the parish rectory. At an evening church service he warmly thanked the people for welcoming him. His charismatic charm captivated the parishioners.

After almost two decades of decline,

leaving the parish buildings in much need of repair, Father Jerry Jakle was appointed pastor of St. Stanislaus Kostka Church in 1971. After six months at St. Stanislaus, the Irish pastor said, "The Polish people have accepted me with open arms. I want to stay here until I die."

Father Jakle had been transferred from another North City Parish, St. Patrick's. A symbol to the Irish of St. Louis, it had once been the largest parish in the city. Reduced to almost nothing, it was demolished. The Shrine of St. Joseph at 11th and Biddle Streets, the mother church of German Catholics, was facing a similar fate.

Working with the Board of Directors, the Irish priest gathered the support of parishioners and other Polish organizations to restore St. Stanislaus Church and to revitalize the parish. Jakle was also serving as the Chaplain for the St. Louis Fire Department, and the church soon became

the site of many of the firemen's ceremonies. Led by Father Jakle, the independent board

◀ Father Jerry Jakle, an Irishman, was loved and admired by his Polish parishioners at St. Stanislaus Church.

◀ Teofilia Chrostowski, who had come to America at age 14, met the then Archbishop of Cracow, Karol Wojtyla, during his visit to St. Stanislaus Church on August 26, 1969. (Photo courtesy of Linda Lawson.)

of St. Stanislaus was able to reinvest in the parish complex, despite the sad condition of its surroundings.

Giant, vandalized, empty hulks of buildings shadowed the parish. By 1972, 23 of Pruitt-Igoe's 33 high rise apartments stood vacant. The buildings still occupied, mostly along Cass, housed 749 low income families. Whether the buildings of Pruitt-Igoe could be adapted, renovated or reused was being debated.

Two of Pruitt-Igoe's 33 buildings were dynamited in 1972.

Three years later, the project was deemed irretrievable and total demolition of Pruitt-Igoe began.

Standing tall in the midst of ruins, gradually, St. Stanislaus Kostka Church was being recognized for its architectural and its historical significance. With many of the early, ethnic churches already gone — like St. Casimir, St. Michael, St. Patrick — and others vacant and threatened, St. Stanislaus Church became an official landmark of the City of St. Louis.

Many members of the next generation of Polish-Americans, though raised in North County, were being brought back to the Polish Falcons Hall on St. Louis Avenue for athletics,

▲ Polish Falcon gymnast Henry Podolski on the parallel bars. (Photo courtesy of the Polish Falcons Nest 45.)

gymnastics, Polish dancing,… The soccer teams, football teams, pompom squads and cheer leading squads of Rosary High School, established in North County in 1960, were filled with the young athletes trained by the Polish Falcons.

A great celebration overflowed St. Hedwig's church and hall in December of 1976 — the dedication of a new shrine. The parish numbered about 500 families. About half of the parish families were of Polish descent. One parishioner, Martha Rutkowska, contributed the entire $35,000 to cast and install a bronze shrine, designed by Monsignor Joseph Baker, against the brick interior wall of the church. The shrine honored a Polish Franciscan priest named Father Maximilian Kolbe. Imprisoned at Auschwitz, Kolbe had given his life in the place of another Polish victim of the Nazis — a victim who had a wife and children.

While doing errands on the afternoon of October, 16, 1978, Ted Sulzer heard on the radio that a new pope had been chosen, but he didn't hear the new pope's name. Sulzer, who had grown up in Sts. Cyril and Methodius Polish National Catholic Church, and his wife Mary, who had grown up in St. Adalbert Parish in North City's Walnut Park neighborhood, had lived in their home in Jennings since 1970. Like the North City neighborhoods where they grew up, their subdivision neighbors included Irishmen and Italians. When Sulzer returned to his subdivision that afternoon, and parked the car in his driveway, retired Mr. Sweeney came over from across the street.

Sweeney knelt down before Sulzer, and began, with his arms extended before him, dramatically bowing to Sulzer. He was saying, "Now I have to bow down before these Polish people instead of the Italianos."

It was then that Sulzer learned that Polish Archbishop Karol Wojtyla had been chosen as the next Pope.

By 1979, parishioners had raised $200,000 for the physical restoration of Stanislaus Church. The statue of St. Patrick was installed in the Polish Church. That statue is perhaps all that remains of that great parish, St. Patrick Church, where the Polish parish had found a home before they could build their own church in 1882. Father Jakle and the parishioners felt the statue was, "…a most fitting symbol both of the support which the Polish community received from other ethnic groups over the first century of its existence and an expression of its gratitude for that support."

That year, the church was placed on the National Register of Historic Places. Annual polka masses — masses accompanied by traditional polka music with a religious theme — became part of the scheduled events. The polka masses not only brought people home to

◀ Young lady gymnasts in formation in the Polish Falcons gymn. (Photo courtesy of the Polish Falcons Nest 45.)

their Polish Catholic Church, but introduced younger people, raised in new suburban areas, to the historic church. And following the polka mass was the annual parish picnic, with all its hoopla.

A steady trickle of Polish immigrants fed the Polish community in St. Louis. Most found their way to St. Stanislaus. Immigrant Margaret Florek was so impressed when she first visited the historic Polish Catholic Church and met a friendly man, pushing a wheel barrow, who greeted her in Polish. She didn't realize it was Father Jakle.

After the strikes and revolutionary fervor in the port city of Gdansk spread across Poland in 1981-2, many spirited Poles were imprisoned, or threatened. Some of them received the opportunity to leave, and came here to St. Louis, and again to St. Stanislaus.

News from the past arrived at the home of Genevieve Rozanski in October of 1986. An Englishman working for an oil company drilling in North Africa called. At first his call was puzzling. He asked for Stanley Rozanski of 1531 N. 17th Street. Forty-four years had passed since Stanley had been shot down over North Africa.

The thoughtful Englishman had found Stanley B. Rozanski's dog tag in North

▲ A parade of young Polish dancers kicked off the annual Polish Falcons Festival in 1978.

▶ Dog tag of Stanley Rozanski, an American navigator shot down in North Africa.

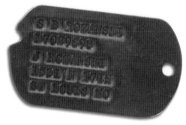

Africa. Not knowing Rozanski's fate, he had searched for him and was attempting to return this momento. Instead, he gave the dog tag of the Polish St. Louisan who had been killed in North Africa to his family.

Though their membership had shrunk, and few lived close to their hall on St. Louis Avenue, the Polish Falcons built an addition to their hall in 1990 — a large, outdoor, wooden pavilion. It covered a floor that could easily hold a hundred dancers, plus scores of picnic tables. With the new pavilion, even in the harsh sun or in terrible rains, the polka music could go on on St. Louis Avenue.

In June of 1993, St. Adalbert Parish was closed. The charming parish complex — church built in 1956, school buildings constructed in 1925 and 1960, and rectory built in 1921— in its village like setting, were sold.

A shrinking, but dedicated, group of Poles continued to worship at Sts. Cyril and Methodius Polish National Catholic Church. They included the younger generation of the Bratkowski family. The family bought several houses on the 1200 block of Hebert Street, saving them from the headache ball. Through their personal work renovating homes, and working with the Old North St. Louis Restoration Group, they were helping to save a few blocks representative of the original, 19th century architecture of that North Side neighborhood.

Parishioners at St. Stanislaus Kostka, led by then Pastor Monsignor Ted Wojcicki, began a development campaign to build a new hall, The Polish Heritage Center. Confident of the parish management, parishioners, businesses and even members of the Jewish community made substantial gifts to this goal. Over a two year period, over $2.7 million was raised.

Archbishop Justin Rigali approved the project and dedicated the ground. On May 19, 2002, Archbishop Rigali presided over the dedication of the new Polish Heritage Center.

While St. Stanislaus parishioners were celebrating the growth of their parish, in the Mount Pleasant Neighborhood of South City, a St. Hedwig parishioner was quietly and anonymously commemorating the past.

Each week, spring through summer, fresh flowers were placed at the grotto at St. Hedwig Parish. A statue of Mary stood in the niche of the limestone grotto, built in the 1930's next to the original school and church. Below the statue, a bronze plaque listed all the young men from the parish who had served in World War II, and the names of parishioners who had died in the War. Year after year, home-grown roses, iris, a spray annuals — kept appearing at the foot of the statue, above the plaque.

Chapter 13

Standing Alone

ulks of once magnificent Catholic Churches — like St. Augustine and St. Liborious — dotted the North Side of the City. Other great and historic Catholic Churches — St. Patrick, St. Lawrence O'Toole, and Sacred Heart — had been leveled, leaving only vacant and weedy lots in their wake.

St. Stanislaus, however, looked almost pristine, it's buildings tuck-pointed, their trim painted. The parish grounds are always groomed. The new Polish Heritage Center opened. The parish, led by their Board of Directors, was restoring all the stenciling and murals on the church interior. Gradually, while the property surrounding the parish was selling cheap, the parish had bought the surrounding eight acres. With the building boom in nearby Downtown, that acreage was suddenly in demand. Including the parish investments and the land, the parish assets were valued at approximately nine million dollars.

Monsignor Ted Wojcicki had won the admiration and affection of parishioners while successfully leading the parish since 1990. The members of St. Stanislaus celebrated Wojcicki being named the new Rector and President of Kenrick-Glennon Seminary, while being saddened that he was leaving their parish. The parishioners knew that Wojcicki had never owned a new car in his life. As a going away present, they surprised him with a cash gift of over $35,000 to buy his first new car.

The Archdiocese replaced him with a young priest who is a canon lawyer, who was to serve as, "Parochial Administrator."

The Board of Directors of St. Stanislaus Parish received an alarming command. After the parish, run by a board for over 110 years, had weathered the destruction of its neighborhood, and was growing and thriving, the Archdiocese wanted to change the way the parish was managed.

Parishioners saw that they were able to

maintain their parish, in spite of what had happened and was happening to parishes throughout North City, because their finances were managed by a civil board, incorporated in 1891. Their board reported to their membership for all the parish expenditures.

The Archdiocese, however, notified the Board that they were to turn the parish property over to a new corporation controlled solely by the Archbishop. In the future, if the parishioners wanted to repair the roof, or restore the frescoes, the Archbishop would have to approve the expenditure of the parishioners' donations.

At this time, the Archdiocese was facing large liabilities related to sexual abuse accusations and criminal convictions of some priests.

The Board of Directors personally petitioned both the Vatican and the new Archbishop, Raymond Burke, to halt the takeover of parish property. In November of 2004, their petition was dismissed.

Meetings between the parish attorneys and Archdiocesan representatives led nowhere.

The priest assigned as parish administrator notified the board that the parish operating funds and an emergency fund totaling

$60,000 had been exhausted by him. He refused to account for any of the money. At the insistence of the parishioners, the Board of Directors took charge of the Sunday collections. The Archbishop disapproved of the Board's removing finances from the priest's sole control. The Archdiocese removed the parochial administrator and his assistant, and did not replace them.

St. Stanislaus Roman Catholic Church, and its loyal, supportive members, were without a priest. Even baptisms and funerals were denied. Each Sunday the parishioners gathered in church, sang, and prayed, and prayed for a resolution.

Meanwhile, Catholics in South St. Louis City and North St. Louis County were in turmoil. The Archdiocese was "reorganizing" or closing parishes. The study commissioned by the Archdiocese for the South City Deaney proposed that a territorial parish should have 1,100 to 1,200 households. Though national or "personal" parishes would be allowed some exemptions from the criteria applied to other parishes, the general and vague description of a viable parish could be used to justify the closing of many parishes — including St. Stanislaus.

There were meetings, protests, suggested closings, new meetings and more protests over the closing of parishes in South City and North County.

In the midst of this, on January 9, 2005 the parishioners of St. Stanislaus made clear their determination to protect the future of their parish. In the new Polish Heritage Center, the parishioners gathered to vote. The question put before them was, "Should we turn over all property, funds and parish control to the Archdioces of St. Louis?"

Bernice Zygmunt Krauze voted. Her childhood memories circled around St. Casimir Parish, which was razed in 1956.

The voting parishioners included Eleanor Deptula Podolski. Like so many members who had grown up in the parish, she had witnessed her childhood neighborhood taken by eminent domain, and destroyed to make way for housing projects.

Adam and Stanley Kaminski and their sister Maria Kaminski Baras were there. Torn from their home by German and Russian invaders, they had built new lives, and raised families here. Much of their spiritual and community life revolved around St. Stanislaus.

Kazimierz Segieda was at the meeting to vote. Sixty years earlier, he had survived Stalin's Siberia and Hitler's armies. He had

▲ Veteran of the Battle of Monte Casino, Kazimierz Segieda, meeting the President of the Republic of Poland, Aleksander Kwasniewski, on May 18, 1999. (Photo courtesy of Kazimierz Segieda.)

found himself a home in St. Louis and at St. Stanislaus.

The vote was decisive — five in favor and 299 against turning over the parish assets to the Archdiocese.

The parishioners then broke into song. 'Stolat," the Polish folk song used to celebrate birthdays, rang through the hall. Literally translated, the song wishes, may you have another hundred years.

June 1, 2005, Kazimierz Segieda was

rushed to the emergency room of John Cochran Veteran's Administration Hospital in St. Louis. The survivor of Siberia and veteran of the Battle of Monte Cassino was suffering from extremely low blood pressure, a life threatening situation. Upon admittance, Segieda informed the hospital staff that he was a Roman Catholic.

The next day, a Roman Catholic priest visited Segieda. His health was still precarious. Segieda made his confession to the priest. Then they discussed the fact that he is a member of St. Stanislaus Kostka Parish, and that Segieda agreed with the actions of the Board of Directors of the Parish, and not with Archbishop Burke. Upon hearing this,

the priest refused to give Segieda the Blessed Sacrament, and walked out of his room.

On June 30, 2005, the Archdiocese officially "merged" or closed many Catholic parishes. Among the closed parishes was St. Hedwig Parish — founded in 1904 by Polish immigrants, and parish to their children and grandchildren. The statue of Mary was removed from the grotto. The plaque, bearing all the names of parishioners who served and died in World War II, was removed.

Ironically, the Archbishop designated a different Roman Catholic Church to be the parish for faithful Poles. An historic German Church, that in recent years had been home to the Latin mass, was to be the Polish Parish — not St. Hedwig, not St. Stanislaus.

In the absence of a priest, the Sunday prayer meetings continued at St. Stanislaus. Secretly, priests had been flown into St. Louis who said mass for Christmas, and Holy Week services. The identities of the priests and their archdiocese were never revealed.

At the annual parish meeting, on August 14, 2005, the hall of the Polish Heritage Center was again packed, and noisy. Journalists, and

◀ The empty grotto of St. Hedwig Parish. After the Archdiocese closed the Polish Parish, the statue was removed from the grotto and the plaque bearing the names of the young men who served and died in World War II was removed. The parish property was sold to another denomination. (Photo by Sheila M. Harris.)

television and radio reporters hovered with their notebooks and microphones.

Having searched this country and overseas for a Roman Catholic priest who would be allowed to serve as their pastor, the parishioners now faced a more challenging decision.

"Should the Board of Directors seek continued Roman Catholic Religious guidance from clergy who may or may not report to the Archdiocese of St. Louis?"

When the votes were tallied, 76 parishioners (22.6%) voted No. Two hundred and sixty (77.4%) had voted Yes.

Quietly, Board Member Robert A. Zabielski and advisor Roger Krasnicki were meeting with a young, Polish born priest. Father Marek Bozek expressed his concern over the parishioners being denied the sacraments, the cornerstone of their beliefs and practices. He, "asked his bishop for permission to take a leave of absence to come to St. Stanislaus to minister to the spiritual needs of the people while the property dispute was negotiated. He was denied permission. Father then gave notice that he was leaving the Springfield Diocese for St. Stanislaus," Roger Krasnicki reported.

Father Bozek arrived in St. Louis on December 23, 2005 to become pastor of St. Stanislaus Kostka Roman Catholic Parish. His first mass at St. Stanislaus was to be on Christmas Eve.

Archbishop Raymond Burke's response was to excommunicate the members of the Board of Directors of St. Stanislaus Parish. He declared Father Bozek automatically excommunicated. He suppressed the parish and declared the actions of the priest and Board to be an act of schism.

Archbishop Burke warned that anyone who received Holy Communion at St. Stanislaus would be committing a "gravely sinful" act.

Many parishioners, and especially board members, encountered criticism, even condemnation, from Catholic acquaintances.

Christmas Eve 2005 — the night of Father Bozek's first mass as pastor of St. Stanislaus — was a bitterly cold night. A piercing mist, made it more bitter. And snow threatened.

That evening firemen parked their huge trucks on 20th Street, in front of the church, and extended their ladders high into the air. From those ladders they hung a huge American flag.

Mass was to begin at 10:30 p.m., but the church parking lots were filling at 8:30 p.m. An hour before mass was to begin, the church was overflowing. People then went to the Polish Heritage Center, where the mass could be viewed by closed circuit television. The hall started to fill up. Then, it too had only standing room remaining. Cars lined the curbs of the streets around the parish for a four block radius. And still people came through the cold and mist. They lined the aisles and crowded the vestibule of the church, and stood in the back of the hall.

At 10:30 p.m., young Father Bozek entered the vestibule of the gleaming, century-old church. The altar boys, before him, seemed nervous, maybe a little jittery with the crowds and cameras. Bozek talked to them in calming fashion, they adjusted the censors, and readied for the procession into the church.

With the choir singing "Silent Night," the altar boys and priest started walking up the aisle. Applause started among the crowd squeezed into the vestibule. As the procession moved up the aisle, the jubilant applause spread through the church like a wave. Then it became a serious, almost chanting applause. Finally it quieted, and mass began.

The crowd attending that mass was estimated to be 2,000 people.

Epilogue

Since the arrival of Father Bozek, the membership in St. Stanislaus Parish has grown to over 550 parishioners. Mass attendance has increased four-fold. The parish has established a new Polish language library and, urged by Bozek, is developing plans to build a Sunday School.

The parishioners, through their Board of Directors, continues to appeal to Rome, that they may be allowed to operate and maintain their parish, as a corporation, as they have since 1891. As of going to press, their appeals are still pending.

Archbishop Burke, through Bishop Leibrecht, sought to have Father Bozek's visa revoked by the Immigration and Naturalization Service. If the visa would be revoked, Father Bozek would be deported from the United States, and again, St. Stanislaus Parish would be without a priest.

Expecting such tactics, the Board of Directors of St. Stanislaus Parish had already hired an immigration attorney and sought to obtain Bozek's religious visa through St. Stanislaus.

▶ Father Marek Bozek celebrated his first mass at St. Stanislaus on Christmas Eve of 2005. Because he was willing to serve as pastor of this historic, Roman Catholic Parish, the Archbishop declared Bozek excommunicated. (Photo by Jerry Rutherford.)

▼ Attendance at Sunday masses at St. Stanislaus quadrupled during 2006. (Photo by Jerry Rutherford.)

The visa was denied and Bozek was given six months to leave the country. The Board and the immigration attorney applied through another means, and Bozek's visa was again denied. Then they began another process to obtain a visa for Bozek.

"But the six month clock for his deportation was running from the initial denial," Board Member Robert A. Zabielski explained. "It was to run out in April. Bozek would be considered illegal and severe penalties would be applied, such as once out of the country he could not legally return for two to three years."

Quietly, without any announcements, the Parish Board of Directors decided to pursue another avenue to assure that Father Bozek could continue to serve at St. Stanislaus. Bozek flew to Poland. There he applied directly at the United States Embassy. Zabielski explained that this strategy was kept quiet because, "the tentacles of the Archdiocese are long and Rome is powerful in Poland."

In Poland, Father Marek Bozek was granted his religious Visa. On Sunday, March 25, 2007, Father Bozek was again celebrating mass at St. Stanislaus Church. Afterwards, Zabielski stated, "St. Stanislaus continues to live."

Scenes from the lives of St. Louis Poles ...
playing in Murphy Park during the Great Depression,
or serving in the Polish Army under the command of
the American Army following World War II.

134

Scenes from the lives of St. Louis Poles …
posing for a wedding photo in a studio, on a front
yard in the Baden neighborhood, or at a parish
picnic.

Scenes from the lives of St. Louis Poles ... standing on the steps of St. Hedwig Church, in St. Stanislaus school yard, or on a sidewalk while leaning against the post of a street lamp.

Sheila M. Harris
served as research assistant for this book.

Notes and Sources:

Sources for the 19th Century, Chapters 1 and 2

Biographical information concerning notable early Polish St. Louisans was found in William Hyde and Howard Conard's Encyclopedia of the History of St. Louis, published in 1899, Thomas J. Thomas Scharf's History of Saint Louis City and County, published in 1883, and Walter B. Steven's histories of Missouri.

Federal census records for Missouri from 1850 and 1860, available at the Main Branch of the St. Louis Public Library, provided information concerning early Polish immigrants to St. Louis.

Information concerning Constantin Blandowski's life and career was gathered from an advertisement published in the May 12, 1860 issue of the Missouri Democrat and confirmed by census information. Articles in the May 24 and May 28,1861, issues of the Missouri Democrat, chronicled the wounding, death, and funeral of Blandowski.

The Union Cause in St. Louis in 1861, by Robert J. Rombauer, published in 1909, contains lists of thousands of men who enlisted in the Union Army in St. Louis in the spring of 1861. The Polish names were compared with information from the 1860 federal census in St. Louis.

Musician Dave Lyon compiled the minutes of early board meetings of the St. Louis Philharmonic, which provided information about Sobolewski's tenure with the orchestra. Sobolewski's professional background is recorded in the 1995 edition of The New Grove Dictionary of Music and Musicians.

Sister Mary Martina Stygar, O.S.F., reviewed the stories of early Polish immigrants in her thesis, Saint Louis Immigrants from 1820 to 1860, for her Master of Arts at St. Louis University in 1937. This thesis includes information translated from the 1925 special edition of the Przewodnik Polski, that had included material on early Polish settlers.

The *Globe-Democrat* of July 16, 1882 reported on the corner stone laying of the original St. Stanislaus Church and School building. The November 13, 1882 issue of the *St. Louis Globe-Democrat* carried a feature on the dedication of the original church and school building. The September 14, 1891 issue of the *Globe Democrat* featured descriptions of the corner stone ceremony for the current

St. Stanislaus Church. The September 12, 1892 issue carried an article concerning the dedication of the current church. Microfilm copies of the newspapers are available at the St. Louis Public Library, Main Branch.

Biographical information concerning the church architects was found in census records.

Julius Trojanowski's police career was traced through the Annual Reports of the St. Louis Police Board. Additional information was found in census records and city directories. Further information was found in the 1910 publication History of the Metropolitan Police Department of St. Louis, 1810 -1910, available at Missouri Historical Society.

Copies of letters proposing the founding of St. Casimir Parish, and a census of Polish settlers in St. Louis were amongst the personal collections of former parishioners of St. Casimir. When the parish was closed in 1956, many clippings, letters and documents from the parish office were given to loyal parishioners.

Building permits on microfilm, in the microfilm section of St. Louis City Hall, provided information concerning Polish families building homes around St. Stanislaus Parish, and about construction of the parish buildings.

Articles related to the tragedy of Agnes Flowers or Agnes Kwiatowski are available in the February 21, 1898 editions of the Post-Dispatch.

The John and Theresa Blaskiewicz family provided information about Agnes, and information concerning the Blaskiewicz family.

Two masters theses provided further background information on 19th century Polish immigrants to St. Louis. The Polish-Born Immigrant in Saint Louis, 1860-1900, a Masters Thesis submitted to the University of Missouri St. Louis, June 1979 by Sister M. Angela Senyszyn, O.S.F. and the History of the Catholic Poles of St. Louis, a Masters Thesis completed in 1938 at St. Louis University by John Stanislaus Mysliwiec, C.R., AB.

Sources for the early 20th century, Chapters 3 through 9

Census records on microfilm at the St. Louis Public Library were the source for all the census data presented about various individuals and neighborhoods. The total figures on Poles in the City of St. Louis are available in addendums to the census records available in the government documents department of Pius the X Libary at St. Louis University.

A souvenir book, Silver Jubilee of the St. Hedwig Parish, (the title was both in English and Polish on the cover) contained names of the founding members of the parish, information about parish organizations, and advertisements that chronicled Polish businesses. The souvenir contains photos and narrative in English and in Polish, and an Honor Roll for World War I. This souvenir is in private collections.

Building permits in the microfilm section of St. Louis City Hall were the source of the information concerning Polish families building homes in St. Hedwig Parish.

Images of the Polish neighborhoods at the beginning of the 20th century were found in A City Plan for Saint Louis, published in 1907 by the Civic League of Saint Louis, and available at Missouri Historical Society.

The St. Louis Red Book of 1911 at the St. Louis Public Library contained information on Polish businesses.

The Carondelet News, available on microfilm at Carondelet Historic Center, contained occasional news items about St. Hedwig Parish including articles concerning the priest selling building sites around the church, the burglary of the parish hen house, and the funeral of war hero Barney Jastrzemski. The neighborhood paper also carried the story of Sergeant Trojanowski chasing the Carondelet chicken thief.

A compilation of memories and history of Our Lady of Czestochowa Church and School, was compiled by a former parishioner, Hania Turek, in 1988. Never published, some of the xeroxed pages are available in private collections. Other data and information is from parish correspondence that is in private collections of former parishioners.

Commemorative Notes, published January 2, 1958 by Henry Tucholski traced the founding of Our Lady of Czestochowa Parish and its closing. These clippings (the name of the publication was trimmed from the clippings) were from family collections. The articles also contain information from Dr. William Swekosky, the chronicler of the demolition of St. Louis architecture during the 1950's.

Further corroborative material was gathered from directories, census records and atlases.

Copies of the letter of excommunication were in the personal papers of families associated with Sts. Cyril and Methodius Polish National Catholic Church and St. Casimir Roman Catholic Parish.

Elsie Bratkowski wrote a brief history of the founding of the Polish National Catholic Parish in St. Louis, that is in private collections.

The development of St. Adalbert Parish was documented through the building permit information, available in the microfilm section of St. Louis City Hall, and old city directories, available on microfilm in the history department of St. Louis Public Library.

The annual report of the Crunden Branch Library, included in the system's annual report, contained the librarians statements concerning the Polish population of the near north side, their habits and characteristics, and library usage.

Missouri Historical Society maintains a collection of biographical data concerning local veterans of World War I. The collection also includes some newspaper clippings and photos. This source combined with information from city directories and census records provided much of the material for Chapter 5.

The Polish Falcons Hall, at 2013 St. Louis Avenue, maintains a collection of news clippings and memorablilia documenting the history of that organization.

Members of the Sutkowski-Bratkowski family and the Krasnicki family shared family memories of Prohibition. Half a dozen other members of the community shared stories of making and distributing home brew, but asked that the family names and names of individuals not be published.

A hard back, sourvenir book, St. Hedwig's Parish — 40 Years - 1904 -1944, for God and Country, commemorated the parish's 40 years and the pastor's 25 years as a priest. The book contained a list of all the parishioners serving in the American Armed Forces and portions of letters from the young servicemen. This souvenir is in several private collections.

Sources for the Post World War II era, Chapters 10 through 13.

The Comprehensive City Plan, Saint Louis, Missouri, prepared by the City Plan Commission with Harland Bartholomew as engineer and presented in 1947, provided data on indoor plumbing and population density in the Polish neighborhoods.

The Zygmunt Family, long-time members of the former St. Casimir Parish, maintained a collection of memorabilia and letters from the last years of the parish. The documents included letters protesting the proposed route of Interstate-70, which took the parish block, and a letter stating the sale price of the parish block, clippings of newspaper articles concerning the closing of the church, and articles noting important events in the history of the parish.

Information concerning the demolition of the St. Stanislaus Parish neighborhood for the Pruitt-Igoe and other housing projects was found in a clipping file concerning Pruitt-Igoe maintained by the history department of the St. Louis Public Library. Pruitt-Igo Action Program, Phase I & II, completed on April 3, 1972, also in the collections of the history department of the St. Louis Public Library, provided additional data.

The Strategic Planning Recommendations for The South City Deanery, Presented to Most Reverend Raymond Burke Archbishop of Saint Louis, December 9, 2004 provided background for the recent struggles of St. Stanislaus Parish. A copy of this study is in the collections of Carondelet Historical Society and the History Department of the St. Louis Public Library, Main Branch.

Saint Stanislaus Kostka Church, 1880-1980, published by the parish and containing a valuable overview of the history of the Polish Parish, is available at the Polish library maintained at St. Stanislaus.

The following individuals in the Polish community of St. Louis shared their personal experiences, family mementos and documents, and family histories for the research of this book.

(While each source is not quoted, each served to corroborate the history of the Polish people of St. Louis.)

Stefania Rakowiecki Amsler, Betty Aurin, John Baras, Maria Kaminski Baras, Helen Jankowski Bauer, John and Theresa Blaskiewicz, Kathleen Blaskiewicz, James T. Bohnak, Thomas Bratkowski, Edmund F. Burdzy, Clare Paszkiewicz Chambers, Darlene Chambers, Dr. Joyce Eisel, Raymond Gawlak, Ted Pienkos-Grywatch, Cathy Jarzewiak Guzdial, Joseph C. Iwasyszyn, Adam Kaminski, Delphine Kaminski, Stanley Kaminski, Walter Kaminski, Marion Kirkiewicz, John Komos, Piotr Kornacki, Theodore Koziatek, Roger Krasnicki, Ben Krauze, Bernice Zygmunt Krauze, Joseph Kuciejczyk, Ben Lapinski, Richard and Sandy Lapinski, John Lewandowski, Jr., Anna Marie Jankowski Mackey, Regina Galkowski Meyerhoff, Ronald Merzweiler, Sister Dorothy Mindak, Bogdan Mirakowski, Audrey Mueller, Paul Thomas Mydler (Mydlarz), Donna and John Nachefski,Susan Pacanowski, Eleanor Deptula Podolski, Stanley Podolski, Stanley Rozanski, Steve Rozanski, Joseph Rudawski, Mike Sawicki, Kazimierz Segieda, Felicia Myslinski Schnittker, Leonard Schultz, John Sobocinski,

Dolores Sokolouski, Henry Sokolowski, Marian Antkiewicz, Spotanski, Barbara Sturman, Joseph Sturman, Mary Sendobry Sulzer, Theodore Sulzer, Sr., Frank Sumski, Milainia Sutkowski Swiatek, Ben Walezak, Bernice Woloncewicz, Florentine Jankowski Wozniak, James Wroblewski.

The following staff members at institutions throughout St. Louis helped in locating pertinent information.

Ruth Brown, Supervisor, and assistants Gloria Carreathers, Barbara Coleman and Jeannie Head of the Microfilm Section of the Comptroller's Office, City of St. Louis.

Ann Grisham, of the Archives Department of the Recorder of Deeds of the City of St. Louis.

Dennis Northcott at the Archives of the Missouri Historical Society.

Steve Czerniewski of the Polish Falcons' Hall.

Lois Waninger, Ron Bolte and Rich Fernandez at Carondelet Historical Society.

Jean Meeh Gosebrink, of the special collections, Mary S. Enns Frechette and Timothy Willman of the fine arts department, Cynthia Millar, Kathleen Smith, Adele Heagney and Noel Holobeck of the history department, and John Mitchell and Keith Zimmer of the periodicals and microforms department of the St. Louis Public Library

Access to the Saint Louis Archdiocesan Archives — which controls the records for the five, historic, Polish Roman Catholic Parishes of St. Louis — was denied to the author of this book.

BOARD OF DIRECTORS
OF
ST. STANISLAUS
ROMAN CATHOLIC PARISH

— CHAIRMAN —

William Bialczak

— PRESIDENT —

Reverend Marek Bozek

— TREASURER —

Joseph Rudawski

— SECRETARY —

Robert A. Zabielski

— MEMBERS —

Stanley Novak

Edward Florek

John Baras

NiNi Harris is a native of South St. Louis City. She has published over 600 articles about St. Louis history and architecture. This is her seventh book about St. Louis. Her works include a history of University City, *Legacy of Lions*, a history of the neighborhoods along South Grand Boulevard, *A Grand Heritage*, *The First Century of Tyler Place Presbyterian Church*, at the heart of the Shaw Neighborhood, *A History of Carondelet*, and *Bohemian Hill, An American Story*. Harris lectures at local colleges, universities and continuing education programs on St. Louis history and architecture.

Jerry Rutherford is a free-lance graphic designer currently based in Boston, Massachusetts, but grew up in St. Louis and has loved to see the steady increase of interest in the restoration of St. Louis. He has participated in the revival of the historic LaSalle Park Neighborhood on the city's South Side and has dedicated his energy and talents to the preservation of St. Louis' heritage by designing *Bohemian Hill, an American Experience* in 2004 and now, *Unyeilding Spirit, the History of the Polish People of St. Louis*.